P9-CEZ-630

PAIN AND PRETENDING

PAIN AND PRETENDING

RICH BUHLER

THOMAS NELSON PUBLISHERS
NASHVILLE

The gender, names, locations, professions, ages, and appearances of the persons whose stories are told in this book have been changed to protect their identities, unless they have granted permission to the author or publisher to do otherwise.

Copyright © 1988 by Rich Buhler

All rights reserved. Written permission must be secured from the publisher to use or reproduce any part of this book, except for brief quotations in critical reviews or articles.

Published in Nashville, Tennessee, by Thomas Nelson, Inc., and distributed in Canada by Lawson Falle, Ltd., Cambridge, Ontario.

Printed in the United States of America.

Scripture quotations are from THE NEW KING JAMES VERSION of the Bible. Copyright © 1979, 1980, 1982, Thomas Nelson Inc., Publishers.

ISBN 0-8407-7627-6

2 3 4 5 6 — 92 91 90 89

TO MY WIFE, LINDA

Parts of the proceeds from this book will be contributed to the following organizations, which are committed to helping children of abuse:

Concept 7 Services for Children
P.O. Box 1745
San Juan Capistrano, CA 92693

CHILDHELP, U.S.A.
Woodland Hills, CA 91367

CONTENTS

ACKNOWLEDGMENTS

If I were to attempt to name all the people in my life who have contributed to my understanding of pain, I would run the risk of leaving out somebody of importance. My thanks to thousands of listeners of my radio program, to hundreds of guests, and to personal and professional friends of distinction who have helped me understand my own pain. Special thanks to my wife, Linda, who has been my partner in the pursuit of truth; to my editor, Janet Hoover Thoma, who has once again arranged all the pieces into a whole; and to the wonderful staff at Thomas Nelson Publishers who have made me feel welcome and excited about writing.

PAIN AND PRETENDING

PART ONE

REALIZING THE EFFECTS OF THE PAST

■

CHAPTER 1

PAIN AND PRETENDING

■

The man on the phone was a well-known minister in our community. I'll call him Dr. Sanderson. He was a dignified, well-educated, and successful man. Although I had never met Dr. Sanderson, I had a lot of respect for him based on what I had heard about him.

"I need to get your advice about something, Rich," he said. "Can we get together right away and talk?"

Later that evening as I waited in my office for him to arrive, I felt a slight sense of anxiety and even some intimidation. He was much older than I, and it seemed that my going to him for help would be more appropriate than his coming to me. I had sensed some emotion in his voice over the telephone, however, so I knew he was not going to talk about business or the mechanics of ministry. Something was troubling him very deeply. What could it be? How could I be of help to someone of his stature?

When he arrived, Dr. Sanderson seemed to fill the room with his presence. I had heard that about him: a dynamic man with an enormous power to influence other people.

"I have been listening to you on the radio, Rich," he began. "I have admired your ability to give straight answers to people with tough problems. I've got a tough problem, and I don't dare talk about it with any of the people in my own church. That is why I wanted to come to your office rather than having you come to mine. I don't want anyone to know about this conversation."

The atmosphere became very still. *This is going to be heavier than I imagined,* I thought to myself. I breathed a prayer for wisdom.

"What's on your heart?" I asked softly.

"My wife and I have had a very difficult marriage," he replied. "We've never really been happy, and we've stayed together primarily because of our children. Now all but one of our children have been launched into life on their own, and our youngest, our only son, is an adult. He is only hanging around home because he hasn't decided what else to do. In other words," he continued, "my wife and I are virtually left with one another, and neither of us considers that much of a bargain."

As he talked and as I struggled to sense the direction of his concerns, I thought, *I guess he's going to ask for advice about his marriage and how to put it back together.*

"About two years ago," Dr. Sanderson continued, "a woman joined our church who had just gone through a torturous divorce, and I counseled her on several occasions. I cannot describe to you how powerfully I was attracted to her. She has a sensitivity I've never seen in anyone and an understanding of deep and complex emotions. I felt so wonderful in her presence that I began sharing some of what I was going through with my own marriage and the longing and the hunger I've had for a better relationship with a woman.

"So far, we have been able to get together without suspicion," he said, "but it has taken a great deal of caution and creativity. She lives alone and can come and go without much notice. I travel a lot, so we normally see one another when I'm out of town."

Dr. Sanderson paused for a moment as if to gather his strength. Then he said, "We are having a physical relationship, and I want you to know that it's the most glorious thing I've ever experienced. I knew my wife and I did not have the kind of friendship and romance that we could, but in my wildest dreams I did not know that what I have experienced in the last six months even existed."

Dr. Sanderson looked straight into my eyes. "You've got to understand what I'm saying, Rich. I'm happier than I've ever been in my life, and I have a relationship with a person who is one of the most caring and exciting people I've ever known."

"I'm hearing you clearly," I replied. "But how can I help you?" My thought was, *Maybe he's gotten to the point where he realizes this has to end, and he wants some advice about how to handle it delicately.*

"My problem is this, Rich. I am confident this woman is the one the Lord has brought into my life to help me with my ministry. How can I most successfully make her my wife and help other people understand what a good thing this is?"

I was astonished. This respected, well-known, veteran minister was asking me how he could dump his wife, marry his girlfriend, and still keep his ministry intact! The man was living in a dream world! In the brief span of thirty minutes he had fallen in my estimation from a distinguished pastor to a confused and deceived man.

I sat for a moment, collecting my thoughts. Was he serious? Had I misunderstood? I decided to continue with his line of thought, just to make sure. "You say you are certain the Lord is in this?"

"I know that sounds crazy," he replied, "but, yes, I am sure of it. I cannot imagine that the Lord wants me to live the rest of my life in the mediocre relationship I have with my wife and to give up my loving relationship with this woman. I have been freer and happier than I've felt in years. Even my sermons have improved."

In my experience people who are pretending this intensely have an enormous amount of pain. Usually the pain has occurred very early in life, and the skill of pretending has been lifelong.

"Tell me about yourself," I said, "especially about your family when you were growing up."

"What's that got to do with all this?" he asked.

"Frankly, Dr. Sanderson," I responded, "I don't think you are handling this very realistically. If you really want my help and my candid opinion, I'd like to request that you allow me to begin by pointing out something to you about yourself that you may not realize."

"All right," he agreed.

For the next several minutes, Dr. Sanderson gave me an overview of his life. He told me where he was born, how many brothers and sisters he had, where he went to high school, how he had decided to go to college and later entered the business world, how he had met the Lord and decided to go into the ministry, and how he had met his wife. He also recited more details about his unhappy marriage.

I was interested in the fact that he skipped over vast portions of his elementary school years. I asked him, "What was the most painful thing that ever occurred to you when you were a child?"

"Nothing painful occurred," he quickly replied. "I have always been grateful for the near perfect childhood I had. It was wonderful."

"Absolutely nothing painful ever happened?" I inquired again.

"Never," he said confidently.

"Dr. Sanderson," I said, "a normal childhood is one with some pain. Each of us has experienced fear, disappointment, loss, and failure of some kind. Nobody has escaped it. Yet you are seriously trying to convince me your childhood was different."

He fidgeted a little, then said, "Well, that's the way I've always remembered it."

"Just for the sake of argument," I said, "why don't you try to recall one tiny moment when something caused you to feel hurt."

Dr. Sanderson reflected for a few moments and then said, "Okay, okay. I remember something unpleasant. When I was about ten years old, somebody stole my bicycle. I was really angry and emotional about it. My uncle offered to buy me a new one, but I was so attached to the one that was stolen that I wouldn't let him do it."

"So there was pain after all," I remarked.

"Yeah, but so what?" he retorted. "What difference does it make?"

"Why did your uncle offer to replace the bike?" I questioned. "Where was your father?"

"I lived with my uncle," Dr. Sanderson replied. "He raised me and my two sisters from the time I was about eight years old."

"Where were your parents?" I asked.

"I don't know," he quickly responded. "I've never had many memories from my childhood."

"The memories are there," I encouraged him. "Just think about it for a moment, and tell me what you can about why you ended up living with your uncle."

After a long time of reflecting, Dr. Sanderson said, "My dad left us. And later my mom died. I guess my uncle was the only one who would take us."

"Do you know why your father left?" I asked. "And do you remember how that made you feel?"

Again he thought for a long time, and then said, "I haven't thought about this for years. It seems as if my mom was sick, and that was why we went to live with my uncle. I remember my father explaining that to us. He said he was moving to a different city so he could get a better job and send us money. After he left, however, we never heard from him again. I don't really know what happened to him."

"This is not turning out to be a very happy story," I said gently. "Are you still willing to say your childhood was perfect?"

With that, Dr. Sanderson's eyes filled with tears. He looked down at the floor and said, "I didn't like living with my uncle. He was an emotionless and rigid man. I don't think he ever really wanted me and my sisters. I couldn't wait to grow old enough to leave him and his depressing farm."

"I'm still curious about your mother," I said. "Why did you have to leave her? What kind of illness did she have?"

Dr. Sanderson sat motionless for quite a while and then began weeping. After a minute or two, he dabbed his eyes with some tissue I had handed him. Then he said, "All I remember is that one day she went berserk, and the police had to be called. Some men came and took her away to a mental institution, I think. We never saw her again. She died shortly afterwards, and no funeral service was held."

Dr. Sanderson arose from his chair, walked to a nearby window, and stood there, gazing outside with a bewildered look on his face. "As long as we're dredging all the junk from my life," he said, "I may as well tell you something else. It's something I have not truly forgotten," he replied, "but until tonight I hadn't thought of it much either."

"What is it?" I asked.

"When I entered junior high school," he said haltingly, "I was befriended by my physical education teacher. He knew I was being raised by my uncle and that I and my sisters had gone through some hard years. He seemed to understand me and offered a lot of encouragement. I felt as if I were very special to him. In some ways he came the closest to being a father to me that I had ever experienced."

Still staring out the window but crying once again, Dr. Sanderson continued, "He began showing me what I now realize was child pornography. Then one weekend he invited me to go fishing with him, and I was delighted. I looked forward to doing something special with him, just the two of us."

Dr. Sanderson lost his composure for a moment, then sobbed, "That was when we started a sexual relationship, Rich. I was so confused. A part of me knew something was wrong with it, but my teacher was so special to me. I felt so awful afterwards I thought I was going to die. I just knew God was going to open a crack in the earth and let me fall into it."

With that, Dr. Sanderson fell to his knees in front of a large, overstuffed chair and buried his head in his hands. Later he told me the molestation by his physical education teacher had continued for more than two years. All this from a man who just a couple of hours earlier had boasted of a perfect childhood.

Dr. Sanderson was what our society has come to describe as a victim. He had been both emotionally and physically abused by his mentally ill mother; he had experienced a great deal of neglect in the care of his uncle; and, of course, he had been sexually abused by his junior high school teacher. Until that evening, Dr. Sanderson had protectively viewed his childhood as perfect and had never realized what he experienced could be called victimization. Even his encounters with the school teacher were something Dr. Sanderson blamed on himself. The guilt from that had been overpowering. As a result, he had begun living in a pretend world, a world where he didn't have to think about all that pain and, eventually, a world in which he actually thought it permissible to divorce his wife, marry his mistress, and try to hold on to his ministry.

That meeting with Dr. Sanderson was a highly dramatic one, and frankly, it is not often that so much happens in a single evening. His story, however, is a fitting introduction to what we want to consider in the following pages: the subject of pain, especially pain in the earliest years of life, and how that affects us and what we can do to deal with it. Dr. Sanderson's story is one of emotional, physical, and sexual abuse, but those are not the only sources of life-crippling pain that can interrupt a person's formative years. Children who have come from alcoholic homes or who have experienced divorce or neglect or the loss of someone in death (or even through significant illness or disability) can sometimes go through the same kind of pain.

I convinced Dr. Sanderson that he needed to talk with a counselor who specialized in abuse and that he needed to confess his problem to his church leadership and ask for help. Dr. Sanderson left the ministry and returned to the business world. He and his wife have put their marriage back together.

Jennifer is another example of what I'm talking about. She was a professional person, an attorney, and had spent most of her life as a single person. At the age of forty-three, she was swept off her feet by a handsome businessman named Bill, and they eventually married. One evening I received a call from Jennifer. "Can we get together and talk?" she asked. "I'm going through something I do not understand, and it's affecting my relationship with Bill."

When we met at my office, Jennifer told me about the conflict that had been going on between her and Bill. She was depressed, he was angry, and they weren't getting anywhere trying to talk about it. One of the problems turned out to be that Jennifer was smothering Bill with some of her emotions and was living in almost constant fear of losing him, either in death or to another woman.

After listening to Jennifer for about an hour, I told her, "A lot of things need to be worked out between you and Bill, and that will take some time and good counsel, but I'm seeing some evidence of destruction in your own life, some deep pain that probably goes back a long way."

"Like what?" she asked.

"I don't know. You tell me. What was it like while you were growing up?"

"I had a fairly good home, I guess," Jennifer replied. "My father was an executive with a foreign electronics company, so he traveled a lot and wasn't home very often. My mother was a school teacher. Other than wishing Mom and Dad would have been at home more often, I had a good childhood."

I continued to gently question Jennifer, and some important facts became evident. She was the oldest child in the family, so a lot of the responsibility for the other children rested on her shoulders, too heavy a responsibility at the age that she was required to carry it. Another important fact was that Jennifer did not feel love or concern from her father at all. He was, in my opinion, an alcoholic.

Until our conversation, Jennifer had never considered her father an alcoholic, and it provided her with an important insight into her early years. Her father was a decent and quiet man, and she never saw him lying drunk in a gutter, but she realized that he drank almost constantly when he was at home and cut himself off from the rest of the family. She remembered numerous occasions when he was so wrapped up in drinking that she would have to take responsibility for what happened in the home. Jennifer felt deep hunger for his attention and deep hurt for not getting it. Without ever having put it into words, as a young girl she came to the sad conclusion that she just wasn't the type of person who could be cared for and loved.

A key emerged, however, when I asked Jennifer how many children were in the family. "There were three of us," she replied. "I had a younger sister and a younger brother. At one time there were four children, but my little sister died."

"Tell me about that," I urged her. "How old was she when she died, and what caused her death?"

"She was about two," Jennifer said. "I don't know exactly what happened. My parents have refused to talk about it through the years. All I remember is that one night she became very ill, and the ambulance came and took her to the hospital. Later my mom told us she had died. My aunt told me several years later that my sister had had some kind of birth defect, but that's as much as I know."

"How old were you at the time?" I asked.

"I was about nine or ten," Jennifer replied.

"How did you react to her death?"

Jennifer sat motionless for a moment. Then she said, "I don't know. I don't remember."

"What *do* you remember about that period of time?"

Jennifer closed her eyes and got a painful look on her face. "I remember the night she got sick. I remember the ambulance coming and my mother crying. I remember a neighbor lady coming from next door to stay with me. Then I remember my mother coming to me the next day to say that my sister had died."

With her eyes still closed, a look of utter despair and anguish came across Jennifer's face, and she rolled into a ball on the couch where she was sitting and began sobbing. She was so overcome with emotion that at times she didn't even seem to be crying, as though the pain she felt was too enormous to let out all at once. For the first time in her life, Jennifer was expressing the deepest pain she had ever felt.

"I was going through a lot of emotions at once," she later told me. "I was grieving over the loss of my sister, which I never had done before. I was hurting over the way I felt about my father and how I imagined he felt about me. I was also blaming myself for the fact that my sister died. When my mother had told me my sister died, I was overwhelmed with guilt and wanted to run and hide."

Jennifer had experienced deep devastation of more than one kind, and it had produced effects that lasted well into adulthood. Part of the pain in her marriage was the result of the unfinished business from those early years, something she had never before realized.

Dr. Sanderson and Jennifer are examples of people who in their adult years are experiencing deep pain and who seem to have obstacles in their lives that stand between them and certain kinds of happiness. Their pain appears to be in the present and related to current issues, but in reality it is rooted in the past, during their early years when their opinions of themselves were formed. Both Dr. Sanderson and Jennifer happen to be victims, one a victim of sexual and emotional abuse, the other a victim of an alcoholic home and a deep personal tragedy. In the pages to come I will touch upon various kinds of experiences that can produce a lifetime of pain. The principles I will discuss can be applied to various painful experiences, but I will emphasize emotional, physical, and, especially, sexual abuse. Let me begin by telling you how my knowledge of pain, and the pretending that seeks to hide it, began and why this subject is a central part of my efforts to help hurting people.

CHAPTER 2

CHILDREN OF PAIN

■

I remember the first time I ever heard about abuse or molestation. A young girl in my elementary school had been briefly abducted and sexually violated. I didn't understand all that had happened to her, but I do recall the school authorities warning us and our parents to be careful. A description of the man and his car was distributed to everybody in the neighborhood. As time went on, I would occasionally hear about somebody being raped or some child disappearing.

I read a lot of magazines when I was young, and some articles warned about the danger that existed for children, including instructions for parents to teach their children how to say no to strangers. We were all told, for example, not to respond to any adult who tried to offer us a ride or who offered candy as an inducement for getting into a car. We were warned not to allow anyone we didn't know to pick us up from school. Because of all that, most of us thought the average molester was a dirty old man who drove a van and prowled the neighborhoods looking for children to kidnap.

In college I learned that a friend of my wife's and mine had been molested as a child by her father. For years to come, I viewed that woman as one of a handful of pitiful people who had experienced a terrible violation. I carried the impression that victims of incest or other kinds of molestation were like lepers on lonely islands somewhere, a minority of people living on the fringe of society. If somebody had pressed me to describe who they were and where they had come from, I would have theorized that they were low income people who lived on the verge of poverty.

I have always had a heart for people who hurt, partly because of the pain I have experienced in my own life. When I entered into ministry, I found great fulfillment by helping hurting people and teaching the Bible to them. I loved seeing the release in their lives as the power of the Word of God penetrated their hearts and their understanding. I came to enjoy the relationships I had with professional counselors to whom I referred people who obviously needed more than just a pastor's genuine interest.

Through the years of my pastoral ministry, I saw a whole range of problems and heard a variety of stories from those who came for help. Some were suicidal, some had eating disorders. Others had marriage problems or frustrations with extended family or struggles with personal failure. Occasionally, I would run into a victim, a person who had experienced sexual, physical, or emotional abuse. It didn't seem to happen often, but whenever it did, I was always reminded of the friend who, during our college years, confessed to my wife about her molestation. In my mind I would think, *Well, here's another pitiful individual who has experienced what she did.*

Then came "Talk from the Heart," a daily four-hour radio

talkshow, which I began together with the Crawford Broadcasting Company in Los Angeles. I started offering pastoral counseling and advice to those who called, doing on the radio what I had previously done in my office. There was an important additional benefit, however. I could invite some of the finest experts on various subjects to be guests. Together, my audience and I could explore the territory of doctors, professional counselors, ministers, and other kinds of specialists. I could assemble a list of trusted referrals for listeners to consult for help.

At first, very few callers ever brought up the subject of victimization, or if they did, it didn't mean anything to me. We talked about alcoholism, anorexia (a condition characterized by starving oneself), bulimia (a related condition characterized by overeating followed by self-induced vomiting or use of laxatives), panic disorders, depression, marriage problems, drug abuse, and addictive behaviors.

One of the ways we on the program determine whether an interview has been successful is to find out how many calls or letters the guest receives in the days or weeks following the interview. When the program first began, a follow-up response of five or six calls was considered fairly good. Ten or twenty calls was very good. Twenty to fifty calls really encouraged us. More than fifty calls was very unusual.

About two weeks after the appearance of my first guest on the subjects of anorexia and bulimia, I casually called her at home to find out what kind of response she was getting. The weary voice on the other end of the line said, "Oh, about a thousand!" I was stunned. Because of the response to the interview, that guest, Jackie Barille, went on to form an entire ministry for people with eating disorders called Inner Development.

That kind of response meant that something was occurring in the real world of real people that I hadn't previously seen clearly. From time to time, the same thing would happen in response to other subjects, which I had before considered to be obscure: sexual addictions, fear and panic disorders, suicide, and especially the whole range of abuse—physical and emotional, sexual molestation and incest. It was not unusual for guests addressing these subjects to receive hundreds of responses after being on our program.

At first, I was delighted that we were able to provide a link between these hurting people and the professionals or organizations who could help them. I speculated that the reason we were getting such powerful responses was that victims were so intense in their need and that there were few places for them to get help. As I continued to invite hundreds of guests on the show who could address those needs, the picture began to come into focus. Our society, and even my Christian-oriented audience, was riddled with victims of various kinds of abuse. More importantly, it also became clear that the majority of people who were experiencing significant hindrances to success and happiness were actually victims.

As I hosted my program, I watched the ways professional counselors approached problems they heard from my callers. Various kinds of guests would talk about fear or anger or compulsive behaviors or substance abuse. Some of those guests, in my opinion, skillfully and wonderfully "connected" with the caller's problem and offered advice that helped. Others, in my opinion, lamely suggested various psychological or religious rituals, most of which the callers had already tried without success. After two or three years of this, I saw that these experts were falling into two general categories: (1) those who dealt with what was on the surface; (2) those who dealt with what was underneath the behavior. Additionally, those who seemed oriented toward uncovering the root of a person's problem were in agreement that the root almost always turned out to be some form of victimization. At first, I thought this was a simplistic conclusion on their part, which had been influenced by the fact that they were preoccupied with their specialty.

After more than forty thousand telephone calls and nearly five thousand guests, however, the subject of victimization rose in my mind from relative obscurity to a place of absolute prominence. I began to realize that I, along with others, had been trained to deal with leaves and shoots and branches in people's lives, even sometimes with trunks, but not with the roots. If a person complained of being tired and lethargic (that's the leaves), we concluded it could be because of depression (the shoots), so we gave all kinds of advice about how to end the depression. Then, we might discover that underneath the depression was anger (the limbs), so we gave advice about anger. Then, we realized that this anger extended back into childhood and was against the person's father (the trunk). Often underneath that, however, lay the fact that the lethargic, depressed, and angry person was physically, emotionally, or sexually abused (the root).

Most powerfully, as I began to realize that so many problems in people's lives were caused by abuse, I gained increased confidence in approaching my callers and counselees and their needs from that standpoint. I began asking callers if there had been any emotional, physical, or sexual abuse in their backgrounds. Most of them said there had been. I began to recognize that often victims had blocked the memory of what had happened to them and therefore were going from counselor to counselor and place to place trying to get help without success. I began to see a pattern of hurting people, some of whom had been through more than one kind of counseling and who had even told their counselors about the victimization, but who had never been dealt with as victims. Instead, their counselors had dutifully written the facts of incest or molestation or physical or emotional abuse in the case record, and then never mentioned it again.

More than that, I realized the evidence of abuse in my own sphere of family and friends, people whom I had tried to help in the past but without understanding or success. I slowly and reluctantly came to see that for whatever reasons, our nicely dressed, nicely educated, and nicely financed society is absolutely permeated with people who have been sexually violated, physically beaten, or emotionally devastated. As one author put it, "If this were a disease, like the chicken pox, we would declare it an epidemic bordering on a national disaster!"[1]

Statistics can sometimes become a blur, and it is not my purpose in this book to document exactly how many people have experienced destruction in their lives, but some of the statistics and studies are worth noting. Reporting agencies and organizations that research sexual, physical, and emotional abuse measure the number of new victims each year in the hundreds of thousands and the accumulated number of victims in the tens of millions. Most of this data is based on actual reports of abuse through police and other protective agencies, but every expert to whom I have spoken says that less than ten percent of abuse is ever reported.

Diana Russell, a sociologist at Mills College in Oakland, California, recently decided to get a more accurate picture of sexual abuse than can be drawn from police reports. She scientifically selected more than nine hundred women at random from the population of northern California and asked them if they had had various categories of sexual experience as children. The results were astonishing to some but not to the experts who had been saying for years, "Sexual abuse of children has reached epidemic proportions." More than half the women (54 percent) said there had been some unwanted violation of their sexual space, either inside or outside the family, by the time they were eighteen. More than one out of three (38 percent) had been molested. The remainder described incidents such as confrontations by an exhibitionist, nongenital intimate touching from adults, or unwanted sexual advances. As expected, Professor Russell found that only 2 percent of the cases of abuse occurring within the family and only 6 percent of those occurring outside of the family were ever reported.[2]

Dr. Mohan Nair, a Harvard educated psychiatrist who is on the staff of the UCLA Medical Center in California and who specializes in child psychiatry, says that the majority of adult mental health problems in the United States are the result of childhood abuse. Dr. Nair says that many who are diagnosed as schizophrenic in their adult years are actually undiagnosed victims of abuse, many of whom have experienced a blocking of the memory of what happened to them. He estimates that victims of abuse who have developed severe symptoms such as multiple personality or splitting from reality will be under professional care for an average of eight to ten years before being properly viewed as victims and offered help from those who understand victimization. He also estimates that only one in fifty victims of childhood abuse realizes the significance of victimization in their lives and receives effective help for it. He also has a concern about the number of children who are quickly diagnosed as "hyperactive" and who are placed on medication but who are actually victims of abuse who have not been identified as such and who are not being offered help as victims. That does not mean every hyperactive child is a victim. Hyperactivity can be caused by other factors. But, according to Dr. Nair, many children who are victims do show symptoms of hyperactivity.[3]

What about the Christian community? Tragically, the incidence of abuse does not seem to be any different. I have interviewed professionals who feel abuse may actually be higher in certain types of religious homes. David Peters, a professional counselor who has worked with victims of sexual abuse, both through public agencies and private practice, quotes several studies and surveys about what is happening in the Christian community in his excellent book, *A Betrayal of Innocence*. One study was conducted by the students of the graduate school of psychology at Fuller Seminary in Pasadena, California. They surveyed more than 150 pastors and Christian licensed counselors on the subject of incest and found that they had dealt with nearly 990 cases. Peters says, "Such figures make it difficult for us to follow our natural inclination to deny that child sexual abuse affects Christians in this day and age."[4]

One researcher has talked to personnel at sexual assault centers, to college counselors, to therapists and researchers throughout the West Coast and Midwest. "They are unanimous," he says, "in their conclusion that the rate of sexual abuse is no less in religious or Christian homes than in the general public."[5]

I have become convinced that the great majority of significantly hurting people in our culture and in our churches are dealing with the lingering effects of victimization and that one of the most important needs among mental health professionals, church leaders, lay counselors, and anyone else who is concerned with the hurting person is to get serious about identifying and dealing with victimization.

DEFINITION OF A VICTIM

First, let me offer a definition of *victim* that will guide us throughout this discussion. In my view, *A victim is a person who has experienced destruction at the foundation of who that person is and in a way that has caused significant hindrance in the living of life.*

The key words in that definition are *destruction, foundation,* and *hindrance.*

DESTRUCTION

In reality, it could be said that we are all victims. Each of us has known and has tasted experiences of failure, unfairness, pain, loss, and torment. No living person has escaped that. As Christians, we also believe the whole world has experienced the effects of sin and has been affected by the disobedience of people created by God. In that sense, this book is for everyone, because each of us has had to decide how to handle that pain. Distinctions exist, however, from person to person related to the cause and intensity of their pain. There is a big difference, for example, between the kind of pain that results from the disappointment of striking out in a baseball game and the pain of being overpowered and sexually violated by another person.

That first kind of pain can actually be constructive,

prompting a person to practice and become better at batting. The second kind of pain is destructive and actually leaves unhealthy debris in the life of the person experiencing it. The first kind of pain was the result of the ups and downs of trying to achieve. The second was caused by the intent on the part of one person to cause hurt to another person. When I refer to victimization, I am talking about the destructive kinds of pain that can occur in a person's life: the devastation, the breaking apart, the dismantling of who that person is because of what has happened.

FOUNDATION

Our discussion in this book will focus on the destruction that has occurred during childhood, the foundational years of life when pain has the most significant and longest-lasting impact. The pain experienced in adult years is no less harmful, and some of it is no less destructive, but the ability to handle adult pain is directly related to how much and what kind of destruction has occurred in childhood. During those early years, a person's opinion of himself is being formed, and that opinion will be the basis of that person's feelings about himself, his decisions about life, and his relationships with other people, including God.

The earlier in life destruction occurs, the more it becomes a part of the foundation of personhood. This is vitally important because our handling of pain later in life is deeply affected by the attitude about pain that we have brought with us from childhood. If, in our earliest years, we have learned that pain is a normal part of life, and we have learned some healthy ways to respond to it, we are more likely to have that same attitude as adults. If in our childhood, however, pain has been overpowering and we have not learned how to respond to it, we are more likely to be paralyzed by it.

HINDRANCE

For many victims, some of the most important experiences of life seem to be out of reach. Obstacles, such as fear and guilt, interfere with relationships, with self-image, with performance and achievement, with happiness. Or destructive behaviors seem repeatedly to halt the progress of that person's life. Once again, each of us has tasted some of this, but many victims' lives are characterized by these hindrances and a seeming inability to overcome them.

Everybody knows what it is like to be angry, but not every person has lost jobs or relationships because of anger. Everybody knows what it is like to experience fear, but not every person has been imprisoned or halted by it. Everybody knows what it is like to feel guilt, but not every person has been immobilized by it. This does not mean that every victim is a person who is nonfunctional or unproductive. On the contrary, most victims have learned to live in the world around them quite brilliantly. But even though success may reign in one area of a person's life, such as school or career, fear and imprisonment may characterize another area, such as personal relationships. Or relationships may seem smooth and problem-free, but school or job is plagued by a frustrating inability to succeed. Or there may be hidden torment, which is evident through strange and uncontrollable behaviors, some of which may be secret. For still other victims, the price may be a physical one, leading to unexplained illnesses.

THE STAGES OF VICTIMIZATION

Many victims are tempted to focus on just one of the major needs in their lives, such as trying to deal with guilt or fear or anger or compulsive behaviors. It is easy for friends of victims to have the same narrow focus and offer simplistic advice such as, "If you would just stop feeling guilty, your life would be perfect." Or, "You need to control your eating, then your problems will be solved." Or, "If you could just trust God, you wouldn't be so fearful."

The fact is, victimization has a shattering effect on the life of the person who has experienced it, and this effect has numerous consequences. I describe the effect and the consequences as a "season of destruction." It doesn't matter whether the victim had a one-time experience, which lasted only ten minutes, or a lifetime of experiences. Since the destruction resulting from victimization took place in stages and the consequences were devastating and sometimes complex, the healing is not going to be a simple process of identifying and dealing with one or two issues. There will be many issues, and each of them needs careful attention.

A season of destruction has five stages: the vulnerability stage, the discovery stage, the eligibility stage, the abandonment stage, and the pretending stage. A question obsesses the mind of the victim at the beginning of each stage. The victim has an intense hunger to find an answer to each of them. For instance, the question that leads into the vulnerability stage is *Who can meet my needs?*

In the second part of this book, we will look together at each of the five stages and explore the feelings and the vulnerability that result from each stage. I have found that victims cannot release themselves from the influences of the pain until they face what has happened to them. Therefore both victims and those who want to help them need to understand the season of destruction.

In the final section we will look at the season of recovery

and explore some of the goals that are an essential part of the healing process. I have talked with multitudes of victims in more than fifteen years as a pastoral counselor. I want you to know, there is hope.

Anyone who is willing to make the effort can experience some measure of relief from pain. Each person's recovery will be unique.

PART TWO

UNDERSTANDING THE SEASON OF DESTRUCTION

■

CHAPTER 3

THE VULNERABILITY STAGE
"Who Can Meet My Needs?"

■

Each of us has a bundle of needs: to be loved, to be approved, to be fed and clothed, to be sheltered. As children, we are usually dependent on our parents to meet our basic needs. As we grow older, we realize that other people—relatives or friends or professionals, such as teachers, doctors, or ministers—are in a position to meet those needs. These are relationships of trust. I have to trust a person before I will allow him or her to respond to my need. To trust someone also means, however, that I am making myself vulnerable. I am allowing another person to be in a position to hurt or to take advantage of me if he or she chooses. We all share this general vulnerability, since it is right and proper for us to count on Mom and Dad or Grandma and Grandpa. No child should experience a violation of that trust. Tragically, however, large numbers of children are victims of the people who are the closest to them. Their abusers have been Mom or Dad or Grandma or Grandpa, and this results in a more specific and intense vulnerability. The child is thrust into the world with needs that are blatantly visible, with a vulnerability that makes that person easier prey for the kind of person who might take advantage of him.

I am reminded of a young woman whom I will call Kathy. I met her while I was the associate pastor of a church in California. Our congregation was not large, so Kathy wasn't hard to spot as a newcomer one Sunday morning. I saw her in the entryway to the church.

"I am from the Midwest," she told me with a smile, "and I'm going to be living here for at least two years while I finish my education. I'm also looking for a good church." She added that she would be returning for our Sunday evening service.

I happened to be speaking that night, and when I walked up to the pulpit, I spotted her right away. I was momentarily startled by what I saw. She was sitting there, arm-in-arm, with a soldier named Chris who had occasionally visited our college group, and whom, I was sure, she had never seen before that morning. I had counseled the soldier on several occasions, and he had a lot of problems. I thought, *This girl has been in town for less than a week and in our church for less than a day, and she has already entangled herself with one of the least desirable characters around.*

A couple of months later, Kathy asked to see me.

"Chris has dumped me," she complained. "I thought we had a good relationship, and now he doesn't want anything to do with me."

"I've been curious about how you and Chris became friends so quickly," I told her. "You were cozy with him from the first day you were at our church."

"Following that first morning service," Kathy replied, "I saw him standing near a table where coffee and doughnuts

44

were being served. I thought he was really good-looking, and since he was in uniform, I thought he might be far from home, so I introduced myself. We really hit it off, and he invited me out for lunch. By the time the afternoon was over, we felt like old friends."

Kathy and I talked at length about how their relationship had progressed from there. They had fallen into a physical relationship almost immediately, even though both of them considered it against their principles, and ultimately Chris had been frightened away by the intensity of Kathy's pursuit of him. He said he had felt smothered by her.

"Kathy, tell me about your background," I asked, "especially your relationships with men."

Kathy got tears in her eyes, and then said, "There have been a lot of men in my life. I guess it's one of my weaknesses. I gave my life back to the Lord about a year ago and have tried to live like a Christian, but people like Chris just seem to have power over me. I feel as if I can't help myself sometimes."

"How early did you begin having sexual relationships?" I asked.

"My first was when I was twelve," she replied. "After that, there were more. I had a 'reputation' in high school."

"Do you have any idea what the root of all this might be?"

"What do you mean?" she asked.

"I mean, you have spent your life almost instinctively getting involved in temporary relationships with the wrong men, usually sexually. That doesn't just 'happen.' Something has caused great destruction in your life, Kathy, and knowing what it is could help you."

With that, Kathy burst into tears and pursed her lips with

45

anger. "All my life I've tried to be good," she said. "I've tried to be a good Christian and have sometimes succeeded for a while. But I can't do it, Pastor Rich, I just can't do it. I always fail. I always do something to mess it up. God must be sick of me."

Kathy and I talked along that theme for quite a while. She had been reared in a highly rigid religious environment. She thought that for God to approve of her, she had to attend church at least twice a week, read the Bible and pray every day, try to "witness" to somebody at least once a day, and try to avoid one of her most frustrating compulsions, which was smoking. Like many victims, Kathy was demanding perfection of herself and thought God was too. As soon as any one of her goals was missed, she would begin a tailspin of despair and guilt and would fling herself in the opposite direction, investing herself in as much darkness and sin as she could find. Then, a few weeks or months later, she would get sick of her sinning, go back to church, promise God that she was going to be perfect, and the whole cycle would begin again.

"Kathy," I told her, "you have to accept complete responsibility for your conduct, and there is no justification for some of the things you've described. But I do think there are explanations for why you are believing such misinformation about yourself."

"Misinformation?" she asked.

"Yes," I replied. "You are believing things about you that just simply are not true, and some of what you believe about God is not true either. It is healthy and right for us to be in church, to study, to live by the Word of God and pray, and to minister to other people. It is also a good idea to quit smoking, because it will affect your health. But, Kathy, the Bible does not say that if you fail in any of those pursuits, God stops loving you."

"I've heard that before," Kathy said, "but I don't seem to be able to overcome all this."

"I think the key is your perfectionism," I responded. "You have a need to be perfect that is so intense, it is ruling your life and preventing you from being able to see things in perspective. Let me ask a very frank question, Kathy, and please be just as frank with your answer."

"Go ahead," she prompted.

"Were there ever any sexual experiences in your child-hood, particularly in your preschool or early grade-school years?"

"Yes," she replied quietly but confidently, "with my step-father. I don't know how many times, but it happened over a period of three or four years.

"My father divorced my mother when I was six years old. I remember that as a very confusing and painful time. Two years later, my mother married my stepfather, and I liked him from the beginning. When he started involving me in sex, however, I felt a lot of confusion again. Later, he and my mom also divorced, and I felt completely adrift."

"Kathy, you don't need to apologize for the hunger you have to love and to be loved and the hunger you have to mean something to a man. Neither do you have to apologize for the fact that you are a sexual being. It seems to me, however, that some important needs that you had as a child were not met in your home. Worse than that," I continued, "one of the people you trusted violated that trust and actually mo-lested you."

I helped Kathy see that she had been released into the world with a vulnerability to anyone who came along and

47

even remotely seemed to be qualified to meet her deep and unmet needs. She had not gotten involved with all the boys in high school because she wanted to have a bad reputation, but because she thought they would give her something for which she was desperately hungry. That same pattern had continued into adulthood.

As a child, Kathy's general vulnerability was the same as everyone's. Because her needs were not met, however, and because those who should have met her needs actually abused her, her vulnerability became more specific and intense. Not every person, however, who goes out into the world with a specific vulnerability has come from a home where abuse has taken place. Sometimes that vulnerability results because certain basic needs simply were ignored at home.

A friend whom I will call Dan is an example of this. He came from a fine home, a Christian home, but his father was a busy and distant man. Despite his love for his father and his father's love for him, Dan was, in some key ways, neglected. He never felt confidence in his father's approval and was unusually vulnerable to men who might offer what Dan really wanted and needed from his father.

"One summer when I was about ten years old, I went to a week-long camp," Dan recounted to me. "The camp had a western theme with corrals, horses, cowboys, and bunkhouses. I was fascinated with the man whom we called the head wrangler. I don't know why, but I needed him to notice me, and I wanted a close friendship with him. I felt like a misfit, a loner at the camp, and I guess I thought if he took special notice of me, I would feel special as a result.

"I began to hang around the trailer where he lived," Dan continued, "and I asked him a lot of questions about the horses. Once, during the afternoon craft time, I made him a special gift and later presented it to him. I can't believe how much I hungered for his attention and how much effort I put into getting close to him.

"At first," Dan said, "the man was polite but distant. About halfway through the week, however, he began to respond, inviting me to help him take the saddles off the horses or to put feed in the troughs. One thing led to another and late one evening, when I should have been in one of the camp meetings, the man took me to his trailer. I was molested by him."

That experience, which Dan kept secret for years, haunted him and changed how he felt about himself. Almost immediately a couple of compulsive behaviors appeared, and he secretly struggled with some sexual problems that his parents would have been shocked to know about. It wasn't until later, when he told his wife and then a counselor about his molestation, that Dan was able to deal with the torment of it. Dan's family loved him, and no one in his childhood home actually molested him. He experienced the loneliness and pain of a form of neglect, however, and the resulting vulnerability set him up for being molested.

This issue of vulnerability is an important one, especially to parents who want to protect their children from harm. Every expert I have interviewed about the abuse of children has said the same thing: The molester looks for kids who will be easily overpowered.

I once received a call from a man who had previously been involved in child pornography. He said he could walk onto any playground or into any video arcade and within a short time would be able to pick out the young people whom he could entice and ultimately trap. He said most of them

were children, especially girls, who felt some kind of aliena-
tion from their parents and who responded to the special
attention he offered them.

I think this message needs to be especially clear to Christian parents. We seem to think that as long as we're committed to our faith and have tried to communicate Christian
principles to our children, molestation could never happen
to them. I heard that just recently from a grieving young
mother whom I happened to meet at a Christian bookstore.
She shared with me the tragic story of the molestation of her
six-year-old daughter. With tears in her eyes she said, "I
didn't think this could happen to a Christian family."

If your children's basic needs for love and approval are not
met in the home, they will be more vulnerable to someone
outside your home. The intensity of that hunger could be
more powerful than their desire to live according to your
standards.

A lot of people are surprised, for example, when a good
Christian teenager "gets into trouble" with drugs, sex, or
other unacceptable behavior. "They should know better," we
say. The fact is, however, that most teenagers who get into
trouble do know better. They know the difference between
right and wrong. They know their conduct is inconsistent
with their own values and the values of their parents and
their God. They do it anyway. Why? Many times it is because of their hunger for love and approval.

A recent study revealed that the influence of the peers of
midwestern teenagers was five times stronger than the influence of their parents! If our children don't get love and approval from us, they'll find them from someone else, and for
some teenagers, they will get what they need at almost any
cost.

One of the most memorable experiences of my years as a pastor is an example of this.

I was at home one evening when I received a call from Mrs. Fleming, a member of my church.

"My daughter, Gwen, is in jail again," she said, crying. "I've arranged bail over the phone, but I need to go to the bail bondsman and give him my money, and then go to the jail to get her out."

"I'm sorry to hear that, Mrs. Fleming," I said weakly. Gwen, who was in her late twenties, had been a heartache to her mother for many years. "What's she in for this time?" I asked.

"She was caught shoplifting," Mrs. Fleming said with sadness. "She was driving my car when she was arrested so I don't have any transportation. Would you be available to take me to the bail bondsman and to the jail?"

"Of course," I promised. "I'll be there as soon as I can."

As I drove to Mrs. Fleming's house, I thought about her family. In addition to Gwen, there were two other children, a boy who was about eleven and a seven-year-old girl. The father was a merchant marine and was gone a lot. I had met him only twice.

When Mrs. Fleming climbed into the car, she didn't seem angry, just sad. She sat quietly on the passenger side and clutched her purse close to her as though it were a teddy bear. She wasn't crying, and I guessed it was because she had been through this so many times before. To me she was like a worn pioneer woman who had resigned herself to a life that was never going to get better and couldn't be worse.

As we drove to the jail, she talked about Gwen. "I don't understand how all this has happened," she said, staring straight ahead. "Gwen was raised in the church, went to

51

Sunday school every Sunday, went to summer church camp, attended a Christian school, and even memorized a lot of the Bible. When she was a little girl, she used to tell all her friends in the neighborhood about Jesus and invite them to church."

As I listened to Mrs. Fleming, my stomach tensed. She was struggling to understand what had happened to her daughter, and yet in reviewing her daughter's life and the influences that had affected her Mrs. Fleming was overlooking something I realized she was probably blind to and didn't understand.

I had been in Mrs. Fleming's home on several occasions, including twice for dinner. Visits to her home were always difficult for me, because I didn't like the way she handled her two younger children. She treated them like slaves, harshly ordering them to do things around the house. Once, during one of my dinner visits, the son was slapped several times in the face for dropping a dish while he was serving us dinner. It was a pitiful scene, and the look on the boy's face showed how scared he was. I accidentally learned of an occasion when the sister was severely beaten. It seemed clear that both children got that kind of treatment on a regular basis. In addition to all this, they were forced unwillingly to have morning devotions and evening prayers. They were systematically destroyed by this kind of treatment, which was obvious to some of the teachers and children's workers at our church; yet at that time we just didn't know what to do about it, something I have grieved over many times since.

This mother, while trying to mold a religious identity in the lives of her children, was abusing and destroying them, and she was blind to the inconsistency and hypocrisy of it all! Her children were among the most vulnerable I have known, and they routinely succumbed to the kind of people who further destroyed them. Mrs. Fleming didn't know it, but Gwen had confessed to me that she had had more than one experience of childhood molestation, one of which was with a relative who lived close by. I have little doubt, now that I look back, that her other daughter had been molested too.

Vulnerability leads to risk-taking. Everyone takes risks in an attempt to meet one's own emotional needs. People like Gwen and Dan, however, are willing to take greater and more specifically directed risks. When their vulnerability is taken advantage of by those they have wanted so desperately to trust, they are ushered into the next stage: the discovery stage, one of trying to figure out what is going on.

CHAPTER 4

THE DISCOVERY STAGE
"What Is Happening to Me?"

■

I live in southern California. When there is a distant rumble or a gentle shaking of the house, one of the first things I think about is earthquakes. One night when I was sound asleep, I felt the bed moving, and it startled me. I sat straight up in bed and shouted, "Earthquake!"

My wife, Linda, who also had been asleep, stirred only slightly. That was my first clue that we may not have been on the brink of disaster. I turned to look in the opposite direction and came nose-to-nose with our family dog, Ziggy, who was sitting on the edge of the bed with a happy look on his face. I realized that the shaking I felt must have been his jumping on the bed, and I felt foolish. During the moment of panic, I had thought not only of earthquakes but also of explosions, thunder, crashing airplanes, and a host of other jarring events. In my semi-sleep, I knew something was going on, but I didn't know what; yet it was important to know so I could determine what I needed to do about it. As it turned out, it was Ziggy, which meant nothing threatening was going on at all, so I gave him a friendly scratch behind the ears and went back to sleep.

On February 9, 1971, the outcome was much different. I had gone to bed late, so at about six in the morning I was deep in slumberland when the small house we lived in started jumping all over the landscape. In addition, an awesome rumbling noise seemed to come from the bowels of the earth. I could hear things falling and breaking all over the house. I was jolted from my sleep but had to fight to arouse myself completely. As I did, dozens of considerations went through my mind.

Our house was located on a hillside so my first thought was: *The house has broken loose of its foundation and is sliding down the hill!* Then I realized we might be having an earthquake. Still wrestling to awaken completely, I ran down the hallway to my daughter's room and grabbed her from her crib. As I headed for the front door with her in my arms, I thought, *Maybe this is the end of the world, and the Lord is coming back!*

Finally, when I got to the front entrance and opened the door, I was faced with a frightening scene. The sun was not quite over the horizon, though the sky was light, and for as far as I could see, there were small explosions all over our community. That's when I thought, *It's an attack! We're being bombed, and a mushroom cloud will form in the sky any minute!* All these considerations ran through my mind in just a fraction of a second as I stood on the front porch trying to evaluate what was going on. I quickly realized that my early suspicion had been correct. We were, indeed, having a severe earthquake. The fireballs I saw were from oil-filled electrical transformers, which had been rocked so violently they had exploded.

The beginning of a season of destruction in a person's life is very similar. A child who has been happily and innocently skipping through the vulnerability stage is suddenly faced with something startling and different. The child instinctively asks himself, *What is going on? What is happening to me?* and struggles to decide what he should do in response. Since many victims have been overpowered by an adult, and frequently a trusted adult, the child is faced with particular confusion. Until now, adults have been people to whom you go when you're threatened or hurt. Mom and Dad have been freely available to cleanse wounds or to protect from bullies. Now, however, there seems to be nowhere to go, no safe place of refuge. The child is caught in confusion. "Should I scream for help? Should I go along with what is being asked of me or required of me? Is this okay? Are there other people who go through this? Is this another of those new experiences of life that is uncomfortable and, perhaps, painful but permissible? Is this wrong?"

For some victims, there is clear evidence from the very beginning that something is wrong. A middle-aged woman named Marion described her molestation at the age of four. "My family was visiting my uncle's farm for Christmas," she said. "I was standing alone in a small orchard near my uncle's barn when my grandfather took my arm abruptly and forcibly took me into a rear door of the barn. I was scared from the moment he touched me because he was being so rough. What happened inside the barn was so frightening and my grandfather's actions were so abusive that I was terrorized. I will always remember the look on his face. The memory of it has tormented me for a lifetime!"

A different story of molestation was told by Sheri. "My father and I had always been very close," she said. "In my later years of grade school he began coming into my room in the middle of the night and would climb into bed with me. We never had intercourse, but there was a lot of sexual contact between us, which he convinced me was okay and very loving and very helpful to him. He warned me not to tell anyone about it, especially my mom. Even though a part of me felt confused and uncomfortable about what was happening, I enjoyed being special to him and was reluctant to question anything about my father.

"This went on until I was twelve years old. By that time, I had developed a lot of emotional problems. A teacher at school saw the signs of victimization and pulled me aside to talk about it. I ended up telling her the whole story, and that started a whole bunch of new problems, but at least it stopped the incest."

Sheri's stage of discovery was prolonged, because it was not clear to her what was happening or what she should do about it. As it dawned on her, however, she felt less and less comfortable with it. She came closer to answering the question, "What is happening to me?"

The effects of the discovery stage vary from person to person and from experience to experience. They can range from mild discomfort and confusion to terror and immediate pain and devastation.

The discovery stage of a season of destruction is characterized by a quest for facts, a straightforward hunger for an explanation about what is happening. Once that has begun to occur, an even deeper need grows in the heart of the victim: to know the meaning of what is happening. This need drives the victim into the next stage of destruction—the eligibility stage.

CHAPTER 5

THE ELIGIBILITY STAGE
"Why Is This Happening to Me?"

■

After being vulnerable and having that vulnerability taken advantage of by a trusted person, after discovering that something very bad is happening, the victim enters into one of the more important stages of a season of destruction. In the midst of the awkwardness and the pain and the aloneness of whatever is happening, another question comes from deep within: "Why is this happening to me?" It is a demand directed toward the sky, toward all people on earth, toward God Himself. It is a request for a computer-like evaluation of all human knowledge, a plea for somebody to sit down with the victim and be able to adequately answer the question, "Why me?"

This is the eligibility stage of destruction. The discovery stage was one of looking for facts. The eligibility stage is a search for meaning. This stage is especially important when we consider that most victims are people who have been abused during early childhood. That preschooler or early grade schooler who is being hurt spends almost every waking moment struggling with the question, "What does

59

this mean about me?" At home, while lying awake at night, while on vacation, or while playing with friends in the neighborhood, he struggles with the question. It becomes a preoccupation and is one of the reasons why some victims are hopelessly wrapped up in themselves.

Some children are fortunate. They have family members or friends they can immediately talk to about what has happened. They can talk about how it made them feel, and they can hear trusted adults explain the truth to them. They can be helped to know that they were innocent.

For most victims, however, what happened to them occurred in secret or within the confidential boundaries of a family that does not allow pain to be revealed. In many cases, victims have actually been threatened about what will happen if they tell. For them it is a private torment, a wrestling match with one of the most important questions of life but without any guidance as to the answer.

"IT'S MY FAULT"

One of the fascinating truths that has come from studying children who have experienced destruction is that they almost always end up feeling personally responsible for whatever happened to them. They feel as though they caused it. They carry personal guilt for it. In some cases the victim has been blamed by the abuser. "If you wouldn't be so hard to get along with, I wouldn't beat you." Or, "It's your own fault, you know. If you hadn't been so sexy and seductive, I wouldn't have touched you." Even in cases where those kinds of statements have not been made, however, most children come away from the destruction feeling responsible for it.

There are scores of examples of this, but one in particular comes to mind: the story of a fifty-five-year-old woman whom I will call Delores. She was referred to me by a close friend of hers who attended our church.

Delores was being pitifully abused by her husband, a fact that her friend had been unable to get Delores to realize. In my conversation with her, Delores said she knew her husband's treatment of her was not right, and she admitted she didn't like it and wanted it to end. But fundamentally, she felt responsible for it. "I'm not a good housekeeper," she told me, "and I'm not always much fun for my husband. If I could just overcome those problems, I think he'd treat me better."

"I'm sure you're not perfect, Delores," I replied, "and there is probably room for improvement in your life, but there is absolutely no excuse for the way your husband is treating you."

"Then why do I feel the way I do?"

"Tell me about your life," I inquired. "How were things in your home when you were growing up?"

At first Delores told me she had a normal home and that she and her parents were close. "Of course, my father was an alcoholic," she added.

I have met few children of alcoholics who have not experienced emotional and psychological destruction. That's why organizations such as Adult Children of Alcoholics are among the fastest growing in the country. Delores, it turned out, was no exception. She had endured both emotional and physical abuse from her father.

As Delores and I talked, however, it became clear that she had spent her entire life blaming herself for her father's treatment of her. Never once had it occurred to her that her father had a problem and that she had not deserved the mistreatment.

"I remember times in grade school when I wished I could die," she told me. "I would lie in bed at night feeling so much like a failure that I believed the world would be better without me. I had failed my father, my family, and God. I would have taken my own life," she admitted, "if our priest hadn't said it was a sin to commit suicide."

Why do children blame themselves? I believe it is because of what I call "the doctrine of eligibility," which exists in a fascinating way in the heart of even the youngest child. We carry this doctrine with us into adulthood, and it affects many of us in ways we may not fully realize. This doctrine prompts a child to conclude, "I am the reason for the pain."

What is the doctrine of eligibility? Quite simply, it is the belief that good things happen to good people and bad things happen to bad people. As we grow and develop, we learn there are "good" people and "bad" people in the world. We conclude that good people are associated with success and victory and bad people are associated with failure and defeat. In simple ways, we learn that to have something good happen in our lives, we have to be good to be eligible for it. We also learn that if we are bad, then bad things might happen to us.

It is important to remember that children are the center of their own world. They don't see themselves as part of their parent's world. Rather, they see their parents as part of their world. Anything that happens in the child's world seems to be telling the child something important about himself or herself.

A child may experience normal victories and normal defeats and learn to view himself or herself in a fair but positive way. Then destruction takes place (molestation, physical abuse, divorce, or even the death of a parent). The child asks, "What does this mean about me?" Many times the answer is, "Something bad, dirty, and sinful has happened to me, and that can only mean I am a bad person, the kind of person to whom those things happen. Otherwise, it wouldn't have happened." The child's view of himself or herself is forever changed. Now that child is the kind of person to whom bad things happen, and that means the child is bad.

This conclusion about one's eligibility usually occurs as the result of a "branding" experience. Even if a series of abuses has taken place, usually a particular one prompted the child to conclude that he or she is bad. From that moment, the child is "branded" with an identity and an eligibility for failure that has a powerful impact on that child's life.

I was born in the West, in Arizona, and my childhood was one of cattle ranches, cowpokes, and Hopi and Navaho Indians. I remember vividly the sights, sounds, and smells of calves being branded. When you think about it, branding cattle is a molestation of sorts. The calf is tracked down, overpowered, forcibly restrained, and branded in a way that causes pain and leaves a mark, which is carried for life. Victims are also branded, and that brand seems to be forever stamped into their self-identity.

This doctrine of eligibility carries into adulthood as well, and we consult it more often than we realize. Can you recall, for example, your reaction when hearing that a friend of yours, perhaps a young father and businessman, was killed in an auto accident or died of cancer? Weren't you tempted to ask yourself, "Why?" Or, "What did he do to be eligible for such an untimely death?" If you arrived home to discover that your house had completely burned to the ground, would you not be haunted by the question, "Why did this happen to me?" Would you not sit and ponder your eligibility?

We often react the same way when good things happen. If I handed you an authentic check for a million dollars, you would be overwhelmed with the question, "Why me?" After confirming that the check was real and was, indeed, for you, you might look up into the sky and ponder your eligibility. You might eventually come to the conclusion that no matter what the explanation is, this surely means something good about you. A memorable scene in the film *The Sound of Music* illustrates this.

The story is about a poverty-stricken, but fun-loving and undisciplined girl who fails in her attempt to be a nun and becomes a nanny for the children of a rich baron. Eventually, the baron falls in love with her, lowly as she is, and asks her to marry him. She is stunned and delighted and stands in the gazebo pondering the meaning of such a wonderful turn of events. Then she sings a song, "Somewhere in my youth or childhood, I must have done something good." Eligibility! Good things happen to good people so I must have done something good to deserve this.

The eligibility stage of a season of destruction, then, is the period when victims come to some important conclusions about themselves and why their victimization occurred. They are tempted to conclude that, since good things seem to happen to good people and bad things seem to happen to bad people, they are bad. That sometimes becomes an inescapable conclusion about themselves. The effects of the eligibility stage are among the most important to understand, and we will deal with them in detail in the next chapter.

CHAPTER 6

THE EFFECTS OF
THE ELIGIBILITY STAGE
Fear, Guilt, and Anger

■

The eligibility stage produces lasting consequences in the life of a victim. Effects can be many, but I will emphasize the most important: fear, guilt, and anger.

FEAR

One of the most common results of abuse or neglect for the victim is a lifetime of fear. Sometimes the fear is specific, such as a fear of men, a fear of public restrooms, or a fear of flying. Other times the fear is not attached to anything in particular. These victims live under an umbrella of dread. It is as though they are carrying a ticket to disaster in their pockets. They are candidates for anything bad that can happen to a person. They think, *If I get on the airplane, it will crash.* Or, *If I take the train, it will derail.* Or, *If I get pregnant, I will lose the baby or it will be sick or deformed.* Or, *If I apply for the job, I will be turned down,* or *If I give my life to God, He will do something awful with it.* This is the result of the feeling of eligibility.

One man whose story I am familiar with is an example of someone who lived with the expectation that whatever is bad was surely going to happen to him. Jeff was a successful, well-educated, and popular person. No one would have guessed that fear was an ever-present part of his life.

"I'm afraid of the dark," he once confessed to me. "I thought everyone felt the way I do, but during a recent men's camp, I discovered that I was the only one in my cabin who was reluctant to walk outside after the sun had gone down."

Jeff had accommodated his fear of the dark by avoiding doing anything outside the house at night. "If I forgot to take out the trash during the day," he told me, "I would have to grit my teeth and do it after dark, but I hated it and felt that something hiding in the darkness alongside my house was going to jump out and get me."

Jeff's fear was not only of the dark. "I live with the constant threat that something bad is going to happen to me," he said. "I frequently experience the fear that I have a dreaded disease and am going to die from it." He said he did not go to the doctor very often, because it frightened him; but when he did he always braced himself for the worst.

"I also experience a lot of threat," he told me. "I'm never secure at work, even though I do a good job and have been successful. I often fear I am going to lose my job or that something is going to happen to disgrace me."

Jeff was living with a sense of fear and dread that had perplexed him for years. For most of his life he had never told anyone what he was feeling, because he thought he was normal and that everyone felt the way he did. As he sought help for his depression, however, it became clear that he was a bundle of emotions, which had very deep roots.

"I feel awful about this," he told me, "because I know

that as a Christian I ought to be able to overcome my fear and live in peace." Like many committed Christians, Jeff had tried almost everything in terms of prayer, Bible reading, and other spiritual disciplines. Because they had not seemed to work, he feared he was either not a Christian or not a very good one.

"There is no lack of power in God's Word," I assured him. "I just don't think that power has been applied to the areas of your life that need it."

"I don't understand what you mean."

"Tell me about your family and your growing up years," I said.

"I had a perfect family," he quickly responded. (There's that word *perfect* again!) "I have always had a special gratitude for my mom and dad and their love for me. I had a great childhood."

"Was there ever any sexual contact between you and another person during your childhood?" I asked straightforwardly.

Jeff sat quietly, his face suddenly flushed. "Maybe," he said softly. His successful and confident countenance turned into the visage of a frightened, tormented boy. Tears came to his eyes, his body twitched, and he started wringing his hands nervously.

"What happened, Jeff?" I asked.

"There was a man in our neighborhood who lived alone," Jeff recounted. "His name was Ted. He was friendly with the kids in our area, and most of us liked him.

"The details are foggy," Jeff said, "but one afternoon a friend of mine and I were invited into Ted's house. I can't recall what happened there, but I do have a vivid memory of having the worst feeling in the pit of my stomach as we left the house. I went home and secluded myself in my room for the rest of the day and most of the evening. I was physically ill and scared to death. A couple years later, the police raided Ted's house, and he was arrested, we were told, on charges of child pornography."

As Jeff talked about this, his body continued twitching and jerking, and he became sick to his stomach. "When Ted was arrested," Jeff continued, "there was a 'knowing' deep inside me that something very bad had happened to me in his house, and that it probably had something to do with pornographic pictures. I have lived with the awful suspicion that, somewhere in the world, perverted people are looking at pictures of me in that context."

There was little doubt in my mind that Jeff had been molested in Ted's house, and that was the root of the struggles he was now having.

"I remember the first night I was ever afraid of the dark," Jeff recounted later. "It was shortly after the experience at Ted's house. I was watching a horror movie on television, and although I had watched things like that before, this time I became fixated with the television and felt the entire room fill with fear."

Jeff always had thought the film was responsible for his fear. Instead the film appealed to it, and, in some ways, seemed to confirm it. From that time on, Jeff lived with almost constant fear.

Once again it is important to point out that not all fear is bad and not all fear is the result of victimization. If you are in a genuinely fearful circumstance, you will naturally be afraid. If the earth starts shaking, the car starts skidding, or you get a letter saying the finance company is going to take away all your furniture, your feeling of fear is normal. Life is a risk! For many victims, however, it is difficult to think of themselves in terms of normal risk. It is difficult for them to say, "Yes, there is a risk to driving on the freeway or having a baby or getting a job or saying 'yes' to responsibility or even stepping outside the house. That's okay, though, because I have about the same chances of getting into trouble as anyone else."

The point is, we don't generally fear that for which we do not feel eligible. Fear is rooted in eligibility. If you ran up to me, for example, and yelled, "Rich, the FBI just came through the front door," I wouldn't panic because I haven't committed a federal crime. I don't feel eligible for arrest by the FBI. If I had committed a federal crime, however, I would have a sense of dread, knowing I am eligible for arrest.

GUILT

Another product of the eligibility stage is a seemingly ever-present sense of guilt, which is the result of feeling personally responsible for what happened. Children often feel this, even when their parents divorce or when someone close to them dies.

I recently received a call on my radio program from a twelve-year-old girl who called herself Heidi. "My parents are separated and getting a divorce," she told me. "I have to choose which of them I want to live with, and I don't know what to do."

No child should have to make that choice, so I could see why Heidi was upset. "I feel I'm having to decide whether I love my dad or my mom the most. I know that whomever I choose, somebody's going to be mad."

I could sense by the way she was talking that Heidi was not only sad about having to decide between her mom and dad, but she was carrying the whole load of her parents' separation and divorce. "Heidi," I said, "a lot of young people in your position feel as if their parent's divorce was their fault. Have you ever felt that way?"

Immediately Heidi started weeping, and it was clear that a deep well of emotion had just been opened. "I have tried to be good," she choked. "I know I have made Mom and Dad unhappy with the way I've acted, but I've tried and tried to do better." Sobbing, she was unable to speak further.

After Heidi recovered a bit, I asked, "Heidi, have you felt as if your behavior has caused your mom and dad to decide to go separate ways?"

"Yes," she replied hesitantly. "I thought if I could be good, they would change their minds."

Heidi was a very precious girl who, like all of us, lived at the center of her own world. She knew something awful was happening in her world, and she had come to the conclusion it was her own fault. It is healthy, of course, for us to be faced with whatever might be wrong in our own conduct and behavior and to pursue genuine repentance and genuine change. Heidi, however, was not feeling anything healthy. In fact, it was her overpowering sense of personal responsibility that prompted her to call me on the radio. A mother and a father were going through separation and choosing divorce, and yet it was the twelve-year-old daughter who decided to call for counseling!

That reminds me of another call I once received from a ten-year-old girl who was struggling with some similar feelings. In fact, it turned out to be one of my most memorable calls on "Talk from the Heart," because the girl put her conclusion into much better words than I did! I'll call her Joan.

"My mommy and daddy and I are living with our pastor," Joan told me. "They are having a lot of arguments, however, because my mommy and daddy don't want to go to his church anymore." Joan was in the midst of all these heated discussions and feeling total responsibility for them. "What can I do to get them to stop fighting?"

How do I encourage a ten-year-old to understand what's going on? I wondered to myself. I struggled to help Joan realize that the conflict between adults was something for adults to solve. After what must have been ten minutes of inadequate utterances on my part, I paused and asked, "Joan, do you hear what I'm trying to say? Do you understand?"

"Yes," she replied confidently.

"What did I just say to you?" I asked.

"That it's not up to me. It's up to them!"

In her brilliant ten-year-old way, she had used ten words to express what I had spent ten minutes trying to say. She understood.

I share those two stories to illustrate that a child can feel guilty just because something bad is happening around her. You can imagine how guilt feelings intensify when elements of abuse create additional guilt. A child who has been sexually violated, for example, will easily carry a lot of guilt over the fact that something sexual has happened. In the case of emotional abuse, the abuser frequently uses guilt as the weapon of destruction, telling the child in constant and graphic ways, "You are a nothing!" The abuser makes it clear that if the child would behave a certain way, the abuser wouldn't be so angry.

One of the more unusual cases of a season of destruction I

have dealt with involved a young man I will call Joel. The seeds of destruction were sown by his parents who had emotionally abused him and his brother and sister. The abuse laid the foundation for another kind of devastation, which affected Joel for the rest of his life.

I met Joel one Saturday morning at a church where I was a staff member. I had seen him walk past the church several times, and because we lived in a small town, I had spotted him on other occasions as well. He was a normal-looking guy, but he always seemed preoccupied. In fact, his manner of walking made him look as though he was on his way to punch somebody in the nose. I was outside the church, putting some letters on the church sign, when Joel walked by. "Hi," I said. Joel turned and with no expression said, "What are you doing?"

"I'm changing this sign," I replied. "I need to put some new information on it about next Sunday's services."

"I used to go to church," he said blankly.

"Don't you ever go to church now?"

"No."

"Would you like to?"

"I don't know," he replied. "I don't think I would like it."

"Why not?"

"I don't know. I just don't think I like church anymore."

"My name is Rich," I said, extending my hand.

"I'm Joel," he said without expression.

"Could I buy you a cup of coffee?" I offered.

"Sure," Joel said with a hint of a smile.

Joel and I spent almost two hours in a nearby coffee shop talking, and I ended up meeting with him on several later occasions. His story was a tragic one.

"I left home when I was sixteen," he told me. "I couldn't

get along with my parents. They didn't understand me. I hitchhiked to get as far away as I could. I had always heard about New York, and I knew it was on the other side of the country, so that is where I headed. I worked there for a while, then went with a friend to Indiana and lived there for about a year."

"What brought you back to California?" I asked.

"I don't know," Joel said. "I guess I just got tired of living in Indiana. It was cold there. I returned to this town because when my father was in the air force, my family lived here for a while. I remember our time here as a happy one, so I guess I thought I could tap into some of the happiness if I came here."

Joel confided that he had tried to commit suicide on more than one occasion, and that his life in the Midwest had been one of living in an underground of drugs, crime, and sex. Plainly, he was a tormented person, but why he felt that way was not obvious. It sounded as if his father was a successful person, and his family had been a stable one. His parents were apparently Christians. He felt distance from his father, but other than that, there did not seem to be any explanation for his torment. I suspected that something destructive had happened in his life, but unless he had repressed it, there did not seem to be any evidence of molestation or abuse.

One day he casually mentioned that he had a handicapped brother. "Tell me about him," I asked.

"He's about twenty now," Joel told me. "When he was about two years old, he came down with a mysterious disease that affected his brain. He's never been able to walk since then, and he's got a lot of other problems too." Joel told me that the doctors thought his brother had contracted a rare virus, which had attacked his brain.

I didn't know anything about rare viruses, but his story did not sound convincing to me. His whole manner of communicating changed when he started talking about his brother.

"How did you feel when this happened?" I asked.

"I was about seven at the time," Joel replied. "I don't remember much except that my brother was in the hospital for a long time, and we thought he was going to die."

"Joel," I said softly, "there isn't any way you could watch your brother go through what he did without some emotion. I would guess you not only felt some emotion for him, but you felt some for yourself as well."

"Like what?"

"Do you remember feeling as if what happened to him was your fault?"

When I asked that question, terror came into his eyes. He was visibly shaken. I had asked the question, of course, because I suspected he might be feeling a general sense of responsibility. As it turned out, however, I had accidentally stumbled across something more significant.

In a few minutes, Joel was leaning over the arm of an overstuffed chair in which he was sitting, sobbing, and choking. What tumbled out over the next couple of hours was a story of deep pain and guilt.

Joel's brother had not been brain-injured because of a virus. Joel had concocted that story and had told it to so many people through the years that he had started believing it himself. In reality, Joel's brother had been injured by a blow to the head. The doctors saw evidence of the injury, but no one had ever been able to explain how it happened. Joel was the only one who knew, but when his parents and others had asked him questions, he had denied knowing anything.

"My brother and I were playing in the garage," Joel finally admitted. "I was having fun jumping off a stepladder my father had set up. Each of my jumps was from a higher step on the ladder. My brother apparently decided to try the same thing, and before I knew it, he had climbed on top of an old trunk and had jumped. I saw him at the moment he hit the concrete floor. I ran over to him, but he didn't move, and that scared me. I immediately felt like hiding. After a few minutes, he regained consciousness, but he didn't cry, and he didn't seem quite right."

Later that night, Joel's brother had a convulsion and was rushed to the hospital. The whole ordeal of his brain injury had begun.

Joel's parents were rigid people, especially his father, and Joel had learned a long time before that there were some things you just did not talk about. He had already started the habit of keeping his thoughts to himself and not "making waves." On many other occasions he had kept important secrets to himself or had lied in order to cover his actions.

"You were already prepared to assume that your brother's injury was your fault," I told Joel. "You had carried so much pain and guilt in your life that you had come to the conclusion that anything bad happening in your world was because of you."

You can imagine the torment and guilt Joel felt when he knew his brother was near death. Then he learned that if his brother did live, he would be handicapped for life. You can imagine how Joel felt when his brother came home from the hospital and the entire family embarked on two decades of being dominated by his needs. You can imagine the personal sense of responsibility he carried whenever he saw his father and mother crying or agonizing over his brother's condition or the expense and the time that was required to care for him. You can imagine the deep pain whenever the story of his injury was told, and his parents said, "Nobody knows what exactly happened." Joel went through hell.

The root of Joel's pain was clear. He had lived in a home where he was not allowed to express his feelings. When something tragic happened, something for which he felt responsibility, he had never been able to admit it. The guilt had been overpowering and had contributed to the dismantling of his life.

ANGER

A common result of a season of destruction is a volcano-like flow of anger. Actually, the feeling is probably better described as rage because of its intensity. Sometimes the anger is obvious, because this person "blows up" or actually hurts others physically. Sometimes the anger is hidden, but the rage has a profound impact on the life of the person who is experiencing it.

Anger can occur during any of the stages of a season of destruction, but I introduce anger here because it almost always originates during the eligibility stage. The anger goes in one, or all, of three directions. Anger is directed toward the person who hurt me, toward myself, and toward various other people in my life.

ANGER TOWARD THE PERSON WHO HURT ME

Sometimes the anger the victim feels is a righteous anger, a feeling that something very unjust has been done by one person to another, and that something needs to be done about it. This is a healthy anger and can lead to some wise decisions on the part of the victim, such as getting help for himself or herself and identifying the abuser and holding the abuser accountable for what he or she has done.

Sounds wonderful, doesn't it? The bad guy does something rotten to the good guy. The good guy identifies the bad guy. The bad guy gets caught. The good guy rides off into the sunset.

The problem is that it seldom happens that way. Yes, the victim often has intense feelings about the abuser. Unfortunately, this righteous anger, the kind that says, "I was innocently wronged," is not what many victims feel.

ANGER TOWARD MYSELF

The most common form of anger in the life of a victim is self-directed. It is the anger of the eligibility stage. Instead of saying, "I was innocent, being overpowered and violated by another person; therefore I am angry with that person and want justice to be done as a result," most victims think, *I am a loser. I am the pitiful reason all of this stuff has happened and is happening to me. For that reason, I am angry with myself.* Instead of the anger being directed in a healthy way toward whoever is actually responsible for my pain, I become a pseudo-savior who tragically carries the sins of that person on my own shoulders.

This is frequently at the root of suicidal feelings. A person wants to end it all because he or she feels hopelessly bad. It is like a scene in which the victim is standing in the witness box in a courtroom and the prosecutor eloquently shouts, "Who is responsible for this awful deed? Who deserves to die?" The victim stretches out his arm and points his finger, not at the abuser, but toward himself. He stands in the presence of his tormenter, of the judge, of the defense and the prosecution, and of the jury, and cries, "I am the one who deserves to die. I am the one who deserves to be punished. I am a disgusting thing."

I will forever carry the memory of the face of a beautiful college girl whom I met while conducting a young adult retreat at a mountain camp. The reason I mention that she was beautiful is because she did not think of herself as attractive at all. Her name was Wanda, and she wrote me a note during one of the sessions of the retreat, asking if she could talk with me privately.

"I'm having an awful time this weekend," she told me later. "I don't feel as if I fit in. I don't feel as if anyone really wants to be friends with me. I'm just sick of myself."

As we talked, it became apparent that Wanda was in a lot of torment, and that she had been for a long time. She admitted she had attempted suicide more than once.

"Wanda," I told her, "I don't think it is natural to hate ourselves. In my experience, there is usually an explanation for these feelings, and there is usually a time in our lives when the feelings started. Do you know when you began feeling this way about yourself?"

With tears in her eyes, Wanda replied, "I've always felt this way. I remember feeling I would like to die as early as kindergarten."

I suspected sexual abuse and asked, "Wanda, did you have any sexual experiences with anyone when you were a child?"

At first, Wanda did not recall anything that could be classed as molestation, but as we talked about it, she began to remember an incident from when she was three or four years old. A man who was visiting her home forcibly took her clothes off and did a variety of sexual acts with her. "It seemed like it was never going to end," she cried. "I hated it and didn't understand what was going on. It also hurt."

This turned out to be a "branding" experience in her life, and introduced a season of destruction, which included other sexual experiences with other people while she was still a child. Did Wanda have anger toward the person who originally did this to her? Yes. In fact, she confessed that she would like to kill him. Was that the only anger she felt? No. In fact, it was not the primary anger she felt. She had not spent the last twenty years or more feeling like the victim of a man who chose to hurt her. Instead, she had spent that time feeling personal responsibility for what happened. She also felt dirty. Without putting it into words, she had spent her life feeling, "You don't deserve to live. You are a disgusting thing. You are the kind of person these bad things happen to, so you must be terribly bad. The world would be better off without you, and justice would be served if you died."

A professional counselor who had special understanding of victims happened to be attending that weekend conference. She and Wanda got together, and Wanda agreed to start seeing her on a regular basis to deal with what was going on inside her. I have heard she is doing well.

THE TENDENCY TO HURT OTHERS

Jenny was a thirty-eight-year-old professional woman who, for most of her life, had run her own business. At the age of thirty-two, her commitment to living life as a single person came to an end when John, an eligible bachelor who was a customer of hers, asked her to marry him. I had the privilege of watching their courtship, conducting their pre-marriage counseling, and officiating at their wedding. Six years later, they were the parents of a three-year-old daughter and seemed to be happy.

"I'm really getting worried about myself," Jenny told me one afternoon. "My daughter, Jennifer, is starting to get on my nerves, and sometimes I feel as if I can't stand her. I'm afraid sometimes that I am going to do something awful to her."

"How long have you been feeling this way about Jennifer?" I asked.

"I guess I have been impatient with her almost from the beginning," Jenny replied. "But in the past several months, my impatience has worsened. I am ashamed to say it, but sometimes I feel like beating her to a pulp or throwing her against the wall. I think a part of me would like to kill her."

"Those are pretty strong feelings, Jenny," I responded. "For parents to get tired, exasperated, or occasionally to feel or do something they wish they had not done is normal. But the depth of your response to your daughter makes me wonder what your own years of growing up were like."

"They were pretty good, I guess, I don't really remember much about my childhood."

"When do your earliest memories begin?"

"I remember junior high very well," Jenny said. "I also have bits and pieces from fifth and sixth grade, but other than that, I'm a blank."

"Haven't you ever wondered why you don't remember much?" I continued. "You've completely lost nine or ten years of memories. It's as though you had no childhood."

"I never really thought about it until John and I got married," Jenny answered. "He seems to remember almost everything from his early years. I always thought it was normal to forget."

80

"It is not normal," I explained. "Probably some very painful events are hidden in all those forgotten years, and I suspect that if we knew what they were, we would have some insight into your response to your daughter."

"I'm not sure what you mean," she replied.

"To be blunt," I told her, "it is very possible you were treated badly during those years. Judging by the fact that your emotions have become so intense now that your daughter is three, I would guess your own third year of life was not a pleasant one."

Jenny thought about that for a minute. "There were some problems in our home," she said finally. "My older sister has been in therapy for about a year. She really went through hell at home. I remember once watching my father beat her and hating him for it."

"How long did that kind of treatment go on?" I asked.

"She says she remembers it from her earliest years."

"And that kind of thing never happened to you?" I inquired.

"No," Jenny answered quickly.

"I remember from your premarriage counseling that there were several brothers and sisters in your family," I continued. "How are they doing now, and did any of them get this kind of treatment?"

"I have two younger sisters," Jenny answered. "Both are well educated and have experienced some success, but both are having serious problems emotionally. I have two brothers as well, both younger than I, and both of them seem to be doing okay."

"Do you know whether either of your younger sisters was treated badly by your father?"

"Neither of them will talk about it, but they got the same

81

treatment as my sister. I was older when my sisters were born, and I saw some of what happened between them and my dad."

"Jenny," I said softly, "you have three sisters. One of them is older than you, the other two are younger. All three of them were at least physically abused by your father and who knows what else may have happened. Jenny, do you really think you were the only one who escaped all that?"

Jenny became teary-eyed and defiant. "Nothing happened between him and me," she said. "Things were different between us. In fact, I was a favorite." She put her face in her hands and began crying harder. The rest of the scene was reminiscent of a courtroom drama where somebody jumps up in the middle of the trial and unexpectedly confesses to the crime. Jenny started venting years of pent-up emotion about her father and the fact that he had, indeed, not only physically abused her, but sexually as well, which was probably also the case with her sisters. A person like Jenny does not often get in touch with such facts in just one evening, but it is important when it happens, and it was a wrenching experience for both of us.

I referred Jenny to a good friend of mine who specializes in helping victims of abuse, and it became clear that her desire to hurt her daughter was rooted in the hurt that Jenny had experienced herself. By getting help, Jenny was able to interrupt that cycle in her family and to spare her daughter some of what she had endured.

There is no simple explanation for why an abused person has the potential for abusing another, but part of the picture can be explained by the eligibility stage of a season of destruction. I've said that a child consults the "doctrine of eligibility" and comes to the conclusion that if a bad thing has happened, he or she is fundamentally eligible for bad things. Victims have an overwhelming feeling of not fitting in with other people, especially those whom they view as "good." A victim may feel like a villain who was driven from town by a mob of angry people. He or she feels anger, guilt, fear, and a desire to even the score.

Prior to being victimized, a child usually feels fairly normal. She experiences normal ups, normal downs, normal successes, normal failures. Some kids at school, at church, or in the neighborhood may seem, to her, better than she is and some not as good as she is, but she basically fits in to some social group or another. She's not without experiences of pain or feelings of inadequacy, but they don't seem to be much different from what other people experience. So she can get past those experiences and once again feel a part of the group.

Imagine, for example, that one day a little girl arrives at school with a beautiful, new white dress, a dress that draws the admiration of the children but also, perhaps, their jealousy. Imagine if one of the children angrily goes to a pool of slimy, black mud and collects a bucketful of it and dumps it all over the little girl. Now she and the dress are spoiled. She is humiliated. All the children laugh at her. She is no longer one of them but feels apart from them, dirty and violated. She feels momentarily overpowered and powerless. She also feels anger, an anger that could tear all those kids to shreds.

What would you feel like doing if you were that little girl? I know what I would feel. I would feel like scraping a handful of fresh muck from my clothes and smearing it on them— one by one! Oh, how good it would feel! I wouldn't have to feel alone in my dirt. I wouldn't have to feel a misfit in my soiled dress. I could make as many of them look like me as possible, and doing so would help even the score. I could hurt them the way somebody hurt me, and at that moment I would not feel so overpowered. I would have power!

No matter which weapon is used, the drive of the abuser is to overpower someone. Sometimes the weapon is sex, sometimes a blow with a fist or a kick with a foot. Sometimes the weapon is words, sometimes emotion. This is why a victim of one kind (such as sexual abuse) can relate to a victim of another kind (such as emotional abuse). The weapons are different, but the destruction and the pain are similar.

In summary, the eligibility stage of a season of destruction is a powerful one. It is entered into by the question, "What does this mean about me?" and includes branding experiences that shape a person's opinion about himself or herself for a lifetime. The conclusion is, "Bad things happened to me and therefore I am a bad person, and I will live with the feeling that I am eligible for other bad things to happen." This produces a lot of things, most importantly fear, guilt, and anger.

CHAPTER 7

THE ABANDONMENT STAGE
"Who Will Help Me?"

■

I haven't kept an official count, but I would guess I have talked with several thousand victims of abuse, either in pastoral counseling or during my radio program. A clear pattern has been obvious to me in the lives of victims, a pattern that demonstrates the importance of this next stage of a season of destruction. It is what I call the abandonment stage.

I have pointed out that the question leading into the vulnerability stage is, "Who can meet my needs?" The question in the discovery stage is, "What is happening to me?" At the door of the eligibility stage, the important question is, "Why is this happening to me?" A victim entering the abandonment stage asks, "Who will help me?"

A small child, overpowered by an adult either physically or emotionally, hurts. From the midst of that pain, the child lets out an anguished cry, which says, "Help! Please! Somebody help me! Mommy! Daddy! Teacher! Uncle! Brother! Anybody! I don't want this to happen anymore. Please help me!" Much of the time this cry for help has never been uttered out loud, but the screaming inside the victim's head is deafening. When help doesn't come, an overwhelming feeling of aloneness and powerlessness results.

This has been the experience of multitudes of the victims with whom I have spoken, but let me give two examples. Earlier I spoke of Wanda, the college girl who remembered being molested by a man who visited her home. She was about four years old when it happened, and the memory was very vivid for her.

"I was alone in a bedroom that opened from the side of our living room," she told me. "The man who was visiting us came to me and said, 'I think it's time to change your diaper, honey.' I didn't wear diapers anymore so I remember thinking, *What does he mean?* He put me on a changing table that was in the room, which my mother used for my younger brother. He proceeded to take off all my clothes and do various sexual things to me.

"I felt very uncomfortable at first, then later felt pain and terror. I remember thinking to myself, *Mom, why don't you come and tell this man to stop?* But Mom didn't come, and I felt angry and increasingly scared. Then, when some of what he was doing began to hurt, I screamed in my head, but not out loud, *Please, somebody help me! Somebody stop this man! Where is my mother?*"

Wanda went through pain, panic, and a feeling of having been abandoned, which had an immediate and profound effect on her life. "At that moment," she said, "I decided that since Mom wasn't going to protect me, I was going to protect myself. I have spent the rest of my life hating my mom. I have never relied on her for another thing." Wanda also said that when her mother did later come back into the house, the man who had molested her explained that he had changed her panties for her because they were wet, and Wanda remembered thinking, *Mom, don't believe him. He's not telling the truth.*" She resented her mom for believing the man.

A similar account came from Leo, a fifty-year-old man who, through listening to my radio program, came to realize that he needed to deal with his victimization.

"It happened at my elementary school when I was in third grade," he told me. "My teacher made me stay after school one evening. He claimed I was not doing well in class work and had told my parents he would help me after school hours and drive me home himself. He forced me into oral sex, and I didn't have any idea what was going on. I thought he was trying to kill me and that I was going to suffocate. During that whole scene, I wanted to cry out for help, and in my own mind, I did, but I didn't say it out loud. I remember realizing, to my horror, that I couldn't count on my teacher, because he was the one hurting me. I also couldn't count on my parents, and I couldn't count on the other people at school. I couldn't count on anybody!"

During the abandonment stage, the victim comes to the frightening realization that nobody will come to the rescue. Until that point, help has always been just around the corner. You could rely on adults, especially Mommy and Daddy, teacher and police officer, minister, neighbor, and relative. Now all that has changed. The world isn't safe anymore. "I got out of bed one morning, just as I had all the other days of my life, only on this day, everything changed," Leo told me.

This is especially true when the victimization takes place at the hands of the people the victim should have been able to trust. At home, Mom and Dad are the ones to run to for protection, but if either of them is the one hurting me, I'm cut loose to fend for myself. At school, the teacher is the first one to rely on for help. At church, it is your Sunday school teacher or your minister. At grandpa's house, it is Grandpa and Grandma. At camp, it is the counselor. In society, it is a police officer. If one of those people is the person hurting you, the effect is devastating.

THE EFFECTS OF THE ABANDONMENT STAGE

The abandonment stage produces many results, but four of them are paramount: destruction of trust, anger toward others, a feeling of powerlessness, and the need to make a vow (of silence, revenge, perfection, or control).

DESTRUCTION OF TRUST

The ability to trust others is delicate and takes time to develop. Children learn whom they can and cannot trust. Even though unexpected and threatening events may happen from time to time, there should always be somebody to trust, a home to which I can run, somebody in my life who cares for me and who will defend me. When, through abuse or neglect, that trust is violated, I come to the conclusion that I cannot and will not trust anyone ever again.

A woman named Vanessa attended a church where I pastored. Superficially, she seemed like a stable person. She was attractive, married to a professional man, seemingly a committed Christian. It became clear over a period of time, however, that she didn't trust anybody. She stayed at an emotional distance from most of us. She went from person to person asking the same questions or seeking advice but without ever trusting anyone to help. Her friendships were intense, but temporary. Eventually her marriage went the same way. She came to me in the midst of her divorce.

"I've noticed, Vanessa," I told her during our conversation, "that you have a difficult time trusting people around you. Have you ever thought about that?"

"Yes," Vanessa answered, "that's one of the things that led to the breakup of my marriage. My husband said I never trusted or relied upon him for anything."

"When did that begin?" I asked her. "When in your life did you start telling yourself that nobody can be trusted?"

"I've never really thought about it like that," she answered. "I always figured I was just the suspicious type."

We talked for quite a while, and Vanessa's story turned out to be a predictable one. "My father was an alcoholic," she told me. "He was always so temperamental that none of us ever knew where we stood with him. He was drunk so much that my sister and I learned not to trust him. He loved us, I think, but he just wasn't available." In addition, Vanessa's mother was verbally and emotionally abusive. She remembers many times when she would arrive home from school to face a verbal assault from her mother. "She would go on and on about how much her kids were ruining her life." Vanessa remembered. "She would scream and yell about chores that had not been done or something that one of us had done to disappoint her. I hated it. I remember sitting there listening to her and thinking, *How can I get out of here? Where can I go?*"

One particular memory seemed to be a branding experience for Vanessa. "I think I was ten or eleven years old," she told me. "We were having a family reunion at our house. My father was a gun collector and kept some of his prized firearms in a huge display case in our den. I happened to walk into the den when my mother's brother, my uncle, was taking one of my father's pistols and hiding it in his camera case. He didn't see me so I softly tiptoed out of the room.

"Later, when my father discovered the pistol was missing, he went into a rage and accused everyone in the house of breaking into his gun collection. Finally, I told him what I had seen, and that I was pretty sure my uncle was the one who had stolen the gun. Dad believed me and called my uncle, but, of course, he denied it.

"A couple of days later, my mother pulled me into her bedroom and closed the door. I had just arrived home from school, and we were alone. She began to yell and scream at me and accused me of lying about her brother. She called me every name in the book and said I was a 'devil' who was trying to cause trouble in the family. Then she lost all control and began hitting me. The look in her eyes was petrifying and hateful, and I remember falling to the floor and putting up my hands in defense. She just kept hitting and kicking and saying hateful things.

"Afterwards, I went to my room and locked myself in and sobbed for hours. I had never felt so completely alone in all my life."

Vanessa said her mother concocted a cover story. "Vanessa was attacked by some bullies on her way home from school," she told Vanessa's father to explain the bruises from her beating. Vanessa didn't even try to protest or to correct the story, because she knew it wouldn't do any good. Then she got into more trouble because her father demanded to know who the bullies were so he could give them a piece of his mind. She went along with her mother's charade, lying and telling her father she didn't get a good look at them. Nothing mattered anymore. The feeling that she couldn't trust anyone remained for a lifetime.

ANGER TOWARD OTHERS

If anger toward others has not occurred during the eligibility stage, a lot of anger develops toward other people during the abandonment stage, especially against those who were in a position to help. Sometimes the victim is unaware of this anger.

A friend of mine named Sharon experienced horrible abuse at the hands of her mother. About seven or eight years ago she called me and said, "I'm counseling with my pastor, and he is really helping me resolve my anger toward my mother." I told her I was thrilled to hear that. Later when we ran into one another at a concert, Sharon said, "I'm happy to say I have settled things between me and my mom, and I don't hate her anymore." Then, just a few months ago, I had occasion to talk with Sharon again, and she shared an interesting story with me.

"I started sinking into depression again," she said. "I was really disappointed because I thought I had completely resolved everything from my past. I had even started speaking at various churches to tell my story of overcoming the effects of child abuse.

"I got together with my pastor again, and he helped me discover that I still had just as much anger inside as before, but it was an anger and resentment toward my father!"

"Why did you resent your father?"

"Because I needed my father to be the 'good guy,'" Sharon replied. "I idealized and idolized him. As I grew up, I described him as the best father in the world, and I really believed that. He did love me, but he did not protect me, and I realize now that I hated him for it. I was so busy, however, viewing him as a perfect father and trying to convince myself and other people of that, I didn't let myself accept the fact that he was unable to solve a serious problem in his home."

"How do you feel about your father now?" I asked.

"I went through a painful period during which I had to be honest about my feelings. Now, instead of idealizing my father, I see him as he really is. I know that he loves me, and I have forgiven him for not protecting me. In fact, I have come to see the hurt and pain in his own life and have offered my understanding. I think he and I have the most honest relationship we've ever experienced."

THE FEELING OF BEING OVERWHELMED

One of the keys to identifying and understanding a victim is realizing that a victim is overwhelmed by things that are not necessarily overwhelming to nonvictims. A victim feels powerless when a nonvictim would not. I am often asked the question, "What's the big deal about being a victim? Everybody has experienced pain. Everyone knows what it is like to be hurt or to be treated unfairly. Every person has had some unpleasantness in childhood. What makes a person a victim?"

The normal child has experienced discipline, but the victim has been beaten and humiliated, often for things that are not even the victim's fault. The normal child has experienced discomfort with people he does not like. The victim has been tracked down, pinned down, imprisoned, and hurt by someone bigger and more powerful. The normal child experiments with forbidden things. The victim has been baptized in evil. The normal child knows fear. The victim knows terror.

The result is that the victim often responds to circumstances differently from those around him. He lives with the memory of having been overwhelmed and the fear of its happening again. He lives in a world where certain situations trigger feelings of being overwhelmed. The victim's seeming overreaction to those situations is sometimes perplexing and frustrating to those who are trying to have a relationship with him.

A young man named Wes came to me to talk about his job. "My supervisor is playing mind games with me," Wes told me. "He's making it hard for me to do my job."

Even though other people in Wes's office had the same opinion about this boss, they were not being overpowered and intimidated by him. Some of them had even gone to upper management to complain.

I decided to be very blunt in responding to Wes. "You and I have talked before and I know you were emotionally abused by your parents." (In fact, Wes had spent portions of his childhood locked in a closet.) "I have little doubt that even though your boss is not doing a good job, and even though your evaluation of him is probably accurate, you should not be completely paralyzed by him. In fact," I continued, "it would be nice if you could overcome your reaction to him, because it doesn't sound as if he's worth losing your job over."

After some time and Christian counsel, Wes was able to realize that the intensity and nature of his reaction to his boss was the result of something inside him—something that did not depend on how bad his boss really was.

A young woman named Rachel is another example. I was first contacted by Rachel's husband, Jim, who came to talk with me about his dissatisfaction with their sex life. "She tries to participate," he told me, "but sometimes she just freezes, and that ends everything."

Rachel knew she had been a victim of incest, but she had

never sought any help for it. She had spent years privately struggling with the feelings toward her father, who had molested her. In Rachel's opinion, she had "dealt with all that." As she and her husband and I talked, it became obvious that her experiences with her father had left her feeling completely powerless.

"But I have read a lot of books," Rachel told me, "and all of them say there are times when a spouse might not feel as hungry for sex as the other spouse."

"What you've read in those books," I replied, "is a description of an average married couple who will occasionally have to accommodate one another's feelings. You are experiencing something different, Rachel. You are not merely saying to yourself, *I don't feel like having sex right now*. You're sucking in your breath and feeling panic and helplessness. For you, some aspects of sex are more than just uncomfortable; they are completely overwhelming. That's because sex was part of the overwhelming experience with your father."

I convinced Rachel to spend a season of her life going through professional counseling and participating in a support group for incest victims, which finally helped her to understand why she reacted to certain sexual situations with a feeling of panic and paralysis.

A list of the persons, events, or situations that can prompt a feeling of powerlessness in victims would fill an entire book, but it is important to understand that this feeling can persist for years after the victimization occurred.

VOW MAKING

An unusual fact about victims is their tendency to make promises as a result of their victimization. This can occur during any of the stages of destruction, but it occurs most frequently during the abandonment stage, when the victim, in pain and aloneness, decides to take responsibility for protecting himself.

Childhood is not ordinarily a time when serious vows are made. Children make promises such as, "I'll never forget you" or "I'll write every day," but they are easily forgotten. A hurting child, however, who is trying to decide what to do with pain, is likely to make vows to the death, promises that are to be honored forever. Sometimes those promises are induced by the molester when he or she threatens to kill the child or somebody close to the child if the secret is revealed. In most cases, however, nobody urges the child to make the vow. Instead, it happens in the child's mind and heart. These vows are as unique as each individual, but they can be broadly categorized.

Vows of Silence

A vow of silence is probably the most common vow. I recently met a woman who was molested by her stepfather when she was six years old and vividly remembers telling herself, *I will never speak of this again*. She kept that vow until the age of forty-three. Another woman who was raped in a public park came away from that experience with the fear that if she ever actually spoke words that described what had happened to her, she would die on the spot. That was, perhaps, suggested by her attacker, but she doesn't remember. Yet another woman who was molested by her fifth grade teacher told me, "After it was all over, I walked out onto the playground and said to myself, *That did not happen, and I will never say that it did*." She was faithful to that commitment until well into her fifties.

Vows of silence are sometimes the extension of the rules of the family. In many homes there is an understood agreement among family members that negative subjects are never to be discussed, and serious problems are to be ignored. Children from these homes, even if they have not been traumatized by an incident, are not likely to tell their parents or anybody else what has happened to them.

Vows of Revenge

One girl who had been repeatedly tormented and physically abused by her father remembered lying on the floor, trying to defend herself from his kicking. She vowed, *Someday I will kill him*. This is a common commitment among victims. They promise themselves, "Someday I will rise up and get justice, even if I have to do it myself." Look at the number of court cases where the abuser has been murdered by the person or persons he was abusing.

Vows of Perfection

Since the victim blames himself for what has happened, it is easy for him to feel that he needs to be "good" or "perfect" either to prevent future pain or to cleanse himself from the debris of the past. One woman, a victim and a well-known speaker on the subjects of physical and emotional abuse, told me she remembered one evening, alone in her room, when she looked toward the sky and said, "I will be perfect for the rest of my life." She nearly succeeded! Another female victim shared with me that as a child she prayed every night, "Lord, please help me be good. I want to be good."

Vows of Safety and the Need to Control

The key word for the victim is *safety*. One of the most powerful vows of the abandonment stage is, "I am not going to hurt like this ever again." And from that point on, the victim directs every ounce of energy, skill, and intelligence to remain safe. This, in turn, produces a need for the victim to be in control of the people and circumstances in his life, because if they are potentially out of control, he or she feels the threat of more pain.

A young professional woman named Roxanne distanced herself from intimate relationships for this reason. She was about thirty years old, successful at her job, very talented musically, and the type who could be "the life of the party." She became an annoyance to some members of her church, however, because it became apparent over a period of time that she preferred to have social relationships with married men. She seldom talked to single men, even though they were interested in getting to know her better. As I watched her behavior, I came to the conclusion that she didn't want friendships with any single men because they were potentially interested in a long-term relationship. That was scary to her, I theorized. She would feel trapped, out of control, and would be risking pain. If any of the married men started showing a potentially adulterous interest in her, she would back off—not only because of morals, but because she started feeling as if she was losing control.

I finally met with Roxanne to talk about this, and I was surprised to learn that she did not fully realize what was going on. In fact, she defended it. "I'm not doing anything wrong," she said. "I'm a friendly person, and I like having friends. It's absurd for anyone to think I want to take her husband away."

I decided to try another tack. "Roxanne, several months ago a young man named Gary tried to establish a friendship with you. He seemed like a quality guy, and yet you didn't give him the time of day. In fact, I've never seen you have anything but a surface relationship with an unmarried guy. Yet you will spend hours talking about deep subjects with the married men. Why, Roxanne?"

"Marriage isn't for me," she quickly responded. "I've decided to remain single. I think God has told me to."

I didn't get much further with Roxanne, but a couple of years later her sister came to me for pastoral counseling. Both girls had been sexually molested by their father and another family member. Roxanne, I was told, had led a very promiscuous life during her teenage years. She'd experienced so many hurts with so many men that she didn't want anything to do with commitment, love, sex, or marriage. She'd given up.

Many victims do just this. They have found no one to help them and no answer to their problem. They truly feel abandoned. Their only recourse is to ask themselves the question of the pretending stage: *What can I do with all this pain?*

CHAPTER 8

THE PRETENDING STAGE
"What Can I Do with All This Pain?"

■

Victimization should not occur. No child's innocence should be so thoroughly destroyed. But when it does happen, when the effects of evil people and a spoiled world descend upon a child, he or she ought to be able to go to Mom or Dad or some other trusted adult and say, "Something bad has happened to me, and I hurt." The child ought to hear words of comfort and an explanation that says, "I love you, and I'm sorry you hurt. Please understand that what happened to you was not your fault. Somebody with a sickness did something that shouldn't have happened." The child ought to experience the confidence of protection and defense from any further hurt, especially from the same person or persons who hurt the child in the first place. The child also ought to be able to express the depth of his or her hurt, guilt, anger, and confusion. The child ought to be assured of God's love, God's comfort, and God's desire to heal that child and to accomplish justice in response to the injustice that has been done.

That whole bunch of "oughts" should happen for the

child, but most of the time, they do not. The child has learned from adults that certain subjects or certain experiences are not to be talked about. Or the child may have tried to say something but was not believed or was threatened into silence by the abuser. Then there are the times when the people whom the child would have most likely told, a parent or other close relative, are the very people who caused the hurt.

What does a child do at this point? Now that the child feels cut off from people who can be trusted, including God, what happens now? Where can the child go? The next stage of a season of destruction is the most significant in terms of the remaining life of a victim. It is what I call the *pretending stage*. The question in the victim's mind is, "What can I do with all this pain?"

When the child isn't able to express the pain and receive comfort, or when the pain has been too overwhelming to endure, the child makes a commitment to go on and live through the next hour or the next day as well as possible. It is a matter of sheer survival. But what is done with the pain and the knowledge of what caused the pain?

The child begins to experience what I describe as pretending. The pain is too much to endure, so the child pretends as though the pain is not there and sometimes pretends that what caused the pain didn't happen. The child begins a desperate inner dialogue that goes like this: *There must be somebody in the world who will love me; there must be someplace in the world where I won't be considered such a pile of muck; there must be someplace where I won't feel the way I feel or won't have to think about what happened to me; there must be somewhere I can go.*

So the child is able to live in another world, a new world,

a world of the child's own construction, a world in which there is, at the least, a minimum of time to think about pain and the facts of what happened and, at the most, a reconstruction of who the child is, who Mom and Dad are, who God is, and what the world is like.

This sounds contrived and even deceitful, but it is a way to survive. I stuff the pain and the knowledge of what caused it down deep inside. I lock it in a sealed room where I don't want to venture and where I don't want to take anyone else. The wound, even though it is not healed, is covered up, hidden. And I set about constructing my new life, a life in which I pretend as though what happened to me did not happen or that I do not feel the pain of it. My old identity is locked in the room of my old world.

I distinguish between two kinds of pretending in the life of a victim: the "child-in-shock pretending," and the "criminal-in-hiding pretending."

The "child-in-shock" concerns a person who was faced with something so traumatic and overwhelming that the event was immediately blocked from that person's consciousness. In other words, it was not voluntary pretending. The child didn't say, "I have thought about this for a while and decided not to think about it anymore." It never got that far. Whatever happened to the child was so painful and unbelieveable that it was not considered to be real. The child essentially went on living as though it didn't happen. It is a form of going into shock.

God has given us the ability to blow fuses in the face of something overwhelming and that mechanism can enable people to survive, but that's the only thing it is good for, surviving, not living and relating to our families and friends. Even though I believe God gave us these safety valves, I don't believe he meant for them to be a permanent way of life.

The "criminal-in-hiding" kind of pretending is what influences a person to develop a lifetime of skills for avoiding the painful truth. As I have pointed out, the victim often feels responsible for what has happened. In the mind of the child, he or she is not an innocent victim but a criminal whose true identity and true history needs to be hidden and protected. That kind of pretending is often complex and contains a fascinating mixture of good and evil.

Some of what I'm describing is illustrated by the story of Dr. Sanderson discussed in chapter 1. His pretending was blatant. He was pretending that his adulterous relationship with a woman in his church was all right, that it was going to be proper to dump his wife, and that he could do all that and still keep his ministry. You could listen to him and think, as I did, *This man is not living in the real world*. That kind of pretending did not originate with his adulterous relationship. He had cultivated his ability to pretend in the face of pain very early in life, and he had chosen a different world in which to live because the real world was too painful to endure. His pretend world was not an insincere world, nor was it an unsuccessful world. He had married, committed himself to business, later committed to ministry, and had, from all outward appearances, "made it." His wife and coworkers would tell you there were hints along the way of his problems, but nothing as obvious as when he reached a stage when the stress of pretending finally caused him to crash and he entered a more visible fantasyland.

This ability to pretend is one of the factors that sometimes contributes to what is known as "mid-life crisis." A person arrives at a point where there is no more energy left to pretend. Pretending is a lot of work. When you are young, you can devote lots of energy to that project. But as you grow older, or just get tired of it all, something can snap. That's why people who snap act in such surprising ways, ways that seem entirely opposite of the standards they previously honored. That's why many of them declare, "This is the most real I've ever been. I feel I'm more 'me' than ever before." They are exhilarated to throw aside the pretending.

I have been describing two kinds of pretending. One is an understandable reaction to overwhelming pain, "child-in-shock" pretending. Any of us could experience this kind of pretending in response to a traumatic experience.

The other is "criminal-in-hiding" pretending in which a person lives an undercover life. This person actually believes his criminal-like identity is a hopeless one, and therefore a pretend world where his criminal identity won't have to be acknowledged has to be constructed so his true identity will be protected at all cost.

The pretending stage of a season of destruction creates numerous problems for victims and for those who love them or want to help them. Let's consider some of the most important ones.

CHAPTER 9

THE EFFECTS OF PRETENDING

■

A season of destruction can be interrupted at any moment, and the victim can immediately enter into healthy recovery. Since that doesn't happen often and since the pretending stage seems to be the only alternative to recovery, most victims spend their lives living in this stage. The effects of the pretending stage help explain a victim's feelings and actions.

LOSS OF CONTACT WITH THE REAL WORLD

Sometimes a victim will pretend part of the time and in ways that may not be much of a nuisance. At other times, a victim may seem to be from another world. Some victims pretend at home but not at work; others, vice versa. Still others pretend all the time. Also, without intervention, pretending can become progressively worse.

Elaine was a haggard–looking woman of about fifty who attended our church irregularly. She seemed to have a wonderful spirit and was deeply committed to God, and I was curious about what kind of life she led. She approached me one Sunday morning to make an appointment for pastoral counseling. "It will have to be somewhat spontaneous," she told me. "I can't make any advance plans because of my husband."

A few days later, she called to say she could be at the church within the hour.

"I'm at my wits end," she began after she arrived. "My husband, Nathan, is acting very strange, and I don't know what to do about it."

"For example?" I asked.

"Well, I got a call this morning from one of his business associates who said my husband's company is in danger of bankruptcy. Things have apparently been bad at the business for a long time, but my husband refuses to see the facts. Instead, he has started doing some really crazy things, like taking off with his secretary in his private jet and disappearing for days at a time."

"Is he using drugs?" I asked.

"Not that I know of," Elaine replied. "I doubt it. He's a health fanatic and has always been opposed to drugs. He just seems to have flipped out."

"How does he act at home?"

"We've always had a strained relationship," Elaine responded. "It has taken all my effort and the strength of the Lord to stay with him. He's very demanding. For example, I can't leave the house without his permission, and he doesn't know I'm here talking with you today. That's why I'm not always at church on Sundays. I'd love to be, but it depends on whether or not I can sneak out without his knowing where I am."

"Has Nathan ever hit you?"

Elaine seemed stunned and hesitated a second before answering. "Yes," she said quietly. "I have been hit often. How did you know?"

"Your husband is treating you very abusively by not letting you out of the house without his permission. He's acting in a very threatened and threatening way, and I have seen that before. So it doesn't surprise me that you are being physically abused as well."

"I don't like being hit, but sometimes I understand why he does it. I aggravate him. I don't think I've been the kind of submissive wife the Lord wants me to be."

"This has nothing to do with submission," I responded. "No matter what kind of improvement you should make, there is no excuse or justification for the way your husband is treating you. It's abusive. It's a serious problem."

Elaine started crying and said, "I'm so relieved to hear you say that. I went to a minister once before about these problems, but he told me I should keep my mouth shut, live a godly life, and submit to everything my husband demanded."

"How long has your husband acted this way?"

"Well," Elaine said, wiping her eyes, "he first hit me just before we got married, but I thought it was an isolated event, and it didn't stop us from continuing with one another. But I think his problems really began when our son was killed."

"Tell me about that."

"That was about fifteen years ago," Elaine continued. "Our son was seven years old. His name was Nathan too, Nathan Junior. He was struck by a car in the street near our home and killed instantly. At first my husband seemed to rise to the need of the occasion. He took care of all the final arrangements and seemed to be strong during the whole ordeal. One thing I noticed, however, was that he never really grieved over it. He didn't cry at any time that I knew of, and I could never talk with him about Nathan's death.

"Over time, there were hints that Nathan was not handling our son's death well. On the anniversaries of the accident, he would act as though nothing had happened. He would not allow anyone to say anything about Nathan Junior's death. Then, about four years ago, Nathan began saying bizarre things, such as that Nathan Junior was not really dead but that he was alive and living in Europe and was going to be returning soon. Since then, a whole range of strange things has been happening, and I think it all began with our son's death."

"Your husband is doing a powerful lot of pretending," I told Elaine. "He's pretending as though his son did not die, he's pretending as though his treatment of you is all right and that it's your fault, and he is pretending as though his business is not failing when, in actuality, it is on the verge of bankruptcy."

"What can I do?" Elaine asked. "How can I help him?"

"First," I replied, "I think it will be helpful to realize that his pretending did not begin with your son's death. He's got serious problems, Elaine, and I strongly suspect that his ability to pretend started a long time ago, probably even in his childhood. Because he is so dedicated to protecting himself from pain, I would bet he is a victim of abuse in his own family."

"You're right," she said. "I don't know all the details because he's never talked about it, but his mother once told me that his father treated all three of their children brutally."

"He needs help," I told Elaine, "and there is no guarantee he will get it or, if he does, that it will solve everything. Still, you can make some important choices yourself right now."

"Like what?" she asked.

"First, I am going to refer you to a professional who specializes in helping women who have been abused and who are feeling imprisoned by their husbands. You need to take some steps to protect yourself and your children."

"But I don't want a divorce," she quickly interjected.

"I haven't said anything about a divorce," I responded. "Even if it is your desire to remain committed to your marriage and to pray for a miracle in your husband's life, you cannot allow the abuse to continue. If there is any chance of your husband changing at all, it will be through your treating his behavior like the serious problem it is.

"I also recommend that you and whoever else is responsible in your husband's company consult a good attorney about what's going on in the business and get some advice as to what, if anything, can be done."

Elaine summoned her courage and took my advice. With the help of a professional counselor, she discovered she was a victim herself, which was one reason she had found it so difficult to acknowledge her husband's problems earlier. Elaine and her children, who, it turned out, also had been abused, moved to a friend's home where they could think about what to do next. Nathan was so furious, he went there one night and tried forcibly to get Elaine to return home. The police were called, and Nathan was arrested. As a result, his treatment of Elaine and the children was discovered by the authorities. In addition, it was learned that he had been taking large amounts of money from his company and squandering it. The top leadership, along with his attorney, confronted him about that and threatened to press charges if he did not submit to professional counseling.

Nathan's whole world fell apart, but he agreed to be hospitalized at a clinic that specialized in helping victims. The subsequent therapy changed his life.

Nathan's story illustrates how his pretending, which began in childhood, applied to his adult living and how it became worse as time went by. This kind of distancing from the real world can occur in smaller and less bizarre ways but can still be frustrating to the person experiencing it and to those around that person. For example, are you the kind of person who just doesn't seem to get certain kinds of work done? Does homework get put aside or housework pile up? Do the bills sit unopened and unpaid, or has it been a year since you looked for a job?

Very often you are protecting yourself from the pain of whatever those activities mean to you. It is painful to think about not having enough money to pay the bills, or it is painful to experience failure in the job market. Sometimes sitting at home and watching television without enough money to live on is less painful than being turned down for a job or getting another job just to lose it. Sometimes the pain is associated with something that happened much earlier in life, such as a parent who constantly told you what a failure you were or who put constant pressure on you about cleaning your room or mowing the lawn. Sometimes avoidance behavior represents the deep pain of childhood molestation or other kinds of abuse. One can have the feeling, "I am not eligible for a pretty house or a good job, so why do anything that might lead in that direction?"

COMPULSIVE BEHAVIOR

We are all familiar with some compulsive behaviors: alcohol or drug abuse, eating disorders, smoking, compulsive spending, sexual addictions, and such things as compulsive hand washing or compulsive house cleaning. It is impossible to list them all. All compulsive behaviors have something in common, however: they occur repeatedly and the person experiencing them feels as if he or she is out of control. Compulsive behaviors can occur every day or even every hour, or they might occur in cycles of every few months.

I believe, as do many psychological and medical professionals, that compulsive behaviors are responses to pain, especially the pain of victimization. A root, a source, seems to fuel the behavior. That's an important fact to consider. Almost everyone experiencing compulsive behavior focuses on the behavior itself and tries to stop it rather than focus on the root of the behavior. Many say, "I am an undisciplined clod who, at all cost, needs to grit my teeth and with whitened knuckles overcome this behavior," without realizing that some deeply rooted and undealt with pain is part of the package. Some counselors disagree over whether the cause of the behavior or the behavior itself should be the focus of counseling. I believe both should be dealt with.

Several stages of a season of destruction contribute to compulsive behavior, but I am discussing it as part of the stage of pretending because whatever compulsions might have existed without the pretending are intensified because of the pretending and are doomed to continue unless the pretending is addressed. It is as though the pretending adds fuel to the fire of compulsive behavior.

Let me offer a definition of compulsive behavior that may be somewhat incomplete but will help us understand it in the context of our discussion. Compulsive behavior is *anything in my world that will help take away my pain*.

Remember, a victim is a person who often has cut himself off from the real world and created another world in which to live. That "other" world is one fashioned according to what the victim considers to be safe and according to that for which he feels eligible. For the victim, both pain and pleasure are redefined and misunderstood. The real world is a place of beauty and variety, fun and pleasure, relationships and friendships. The real world is a place of God's design, where it is possible to have a relationship with him. The pretend world becomes a confining place where there is little true pleasure or fulfillment. The limited pleasure that is available becomes addictive and unhealthy.

To illustrate this, imagine a beautiful country, a vast country, with rivers, lakes, trees, meadows, and mountains. A person could roam the fields, swim in the rivers and lakes, eat a wide variety of foods, tame and have friendships with some of the animals, and enjoy life. Dangers exist in this country too, though, such as wild animals, occasional storms, poisonous plants, and the chance of accident. Ordinarily, a person would be able to learn how to live with the dangers. He would build a shelter from the storms, learn which animals are dangerous and which plants are poisonous, and learn how to avoid or recover from accidents. In other words, he would learn to deal with the risks, knowing that most of them are manageable. Imagine, however, that a child is placed in this country alone. Imagine, too, that something frightening, devastating, and overpowering happens when the child is alone, without any adult to protect him or to explain to him what is happening, something such as being surprised and attacked by a lion and perhaps actually bitten by the lion! What would that child do or think? He would instinctively seek protection. Perhaps the child would crawl to a cave or tremblingly construct a small hut in which to live and protect himself.

After a while the child would conclude that it isn't worth going outside. There is too much pain and risk out there. So the child would settle into his hut or his cave with whatever limited food and water was available there and would go about the business of living life. That small enclosure would actually become the child's world. Pitiful as it may seem, it would be a comfortable place for the child, because to him comfort is defined as anything safe. As it turns out, however, pain exists in his little world too. There is the pain of eligibility: "Why did this happen to me?" There is the pain of concluding that it happened because he deserved it and that he must be a terribly bad person to have been treated so badly and to have been bitten by the lion.

So the child looks for something to take away the pain. He looks for something to satisfy his hunger for meaning, for fun, for pleasure. In the real world he would be able to find attention for his wound. He would be able to experience the variety, the meaning, and even the pleasure for which he hungers. In his limited world, however, virtually nothing is available to him. Whatever is available, then, becomes his sources either for the satisfaction of his hunger or for the easing of his pain. As he looks around, he sees that his world consists of little other than his own body. Functions like eating, sleeping, or sexual pleasure, which outside his confinement would simply be a part of his world, now *become* his world. Within this tiny world where he feels worthless and ineligible for anything good, he commits himself compulsively to the only forms of dealing with pain and experiencing pleasure he can find.

Additionally, he might start creating a world of his own, a pretend world in which things are not so bad. Instead of roaming the fields and the mountains outside his hut, he explores the fertile plains of his imagination. In his pretend world, he can be anything he wants to be or do anything he wants to do or have a relationship with anyone he wishes.

Compulsive behavior is more complex than this description suggests, but it provides a good picture of why this kind of behavior is so intense and difficult to overcome. Compulsive behavior is a pitiful substitute, in a small pretend world, for real meaning and pleasure, yet it dulls the pain of the past.

All compulsive behavior is self-destructive to some extent because it isn't healthy, but some of it is more pointedly so. Often a compulsive person feels eligible only for bad; he becomes his own judge and jury, and sentences himself to punishment, such as self-inflicted pain. In addition, the actual type of compulsive behavior chosen might be influenced by the feeling of eligibility. Persons who have been sexually abused, for example, will frequently end up with sexual compulsions. At other times the compulsion may be driven by a need to cause pain to another person.

ERASURE OF THE BRANDING EXPERIENCE

As I've already described, there are occasions in the lives of many victims when painful experiences have been wiped from their conscious memory. Even if some pain is recalled and even if the person can remember enough to be able to say, "I am a victim," it is not uncommon for what I call the "branding experience," or the most painful and significant event in the victim's life, to be erased. Many hurting people have courageously dealt with all that they remember and are frustrated that some of the symptoms of victimization are still just as present and just as strong in their lives. That is sometimes because there is more to remember—in fact, the most important memory may not have yet been uncovered and dealt with.

Not long ago, I received a letter from an irate mother whose forty-year-old daughter only recently had recalled being molested by her father when she was a small girl. The mother wrote, "That's absurd. How could anyone forget being raped?" The fact is, it is fairly common for a victim of abuse to significantly or completely block out the memory of where or how or with whom the pain originated. There is a critical need for this phenomenon to be better understood among pastors and counselors. A large number of hurting people have invested enormous energy trying to get well without success, but they could experience dramatic improvement if the root of their pain were uncovered and dealt with.

When it comes to memories, I believe there are four types of victims: (1) those who completely remember what happened and who call it what it is, (2) those who remember but who have never called it what it is, (3) those who could remember if prompted but haven't thought about it for a while, and (4) those who have partially or completely blocked the memory of what happened.

THOSE WHO COMPLETELY REMEMBER AND CALL IT WHAT IT IS

These are the victims who, if asked, immediately and confidently say, "Yes, that's me." They have entered into the real world enough to know what happened, with whom it happened, and what kind of effect it had on them. These are people who may have already received some kind of help or encouragement or at least have learned enough about what they experienced to deal with it in a healthy way.

THOSE WHO REMEMBER BUT HAVE NEVER
CALLED IT WHAT IT IS

Many people fall into this category, either because they think what happened to them was their fault or because they haven't realized that what happened could be considered abuse.

Maria, a woman of about fifty and a devout Christian, called me one afternoon when I was on the staff of a church in southern California. "I don't feel comfortable talking with my pastor about this," she told me over the phone, "and my daughter said you have helped her, so I'd like to talk with you."

When Maria arrived, she was a nervous wreck and had her daughter with her for moral support. She wanted to talk with me alone, however, so we went into my office and closed the door.

"I don't know how to say this," she said nervously. "It's about my husband. I don't like some of the things he does to me in bed, and I don't want him to do them anymore. I am worried about what God must think of me."

"Maria," I said, "I don't want a graphic discussion about how you and your husband make love, but to help me understand what you're talking about, you will have to give me an example of what you mean."

She seemed at a loss for words and said haltingly, "You know, he always wants to touch me."

"In what way?" I asked.

Maria was at a loss for words. "He wants to touch me here, and here," she said, pointing to her blouse and her skirt. I asked several more questions and tried to determine whether Maria's husband was being insensitive to her feelings or was being brutal with her, but as near as I could tell, she was describing what I would consider to be normal attempts on the part of a normal husband to have a normal sexual relationship with his wife.

"Maria," I said gently, "do you feel that it is wrong for your husband to touch you?"

Maria nervously looked to the floor and was wringing a handkerchief in her hands. "Well, it is, isn't it?" she asked.

As we talked further, it became clear that Maria believed sex was reserved for the purpose of having children, and that even then it was supposed to be a quick, functional act. For all her married life, she had never allowed her husband to do much more than that, and she viewed her husband's romantic attempts as evidence that he was an evil man.

First I took Maria to the Scriptures. I showed her how much God approved of the sexual relationship in marriage and the fact that he designed it and that he told married couples not to withhold themselves from one another physically. I took her to the book of the Song of Solomon and the explicit descriptions of a loving, sensuous relationship. She was astonished. She and her husband were two wonderful but simple people who had committed themselves to the tradition of their own historic church, but who were living in a lot of ignorance about life and the Bible.

I was curious, though, about what had contributed to such a limited view of a married physical relationship. I suspected that Maria not only had grown up with a family who conveyed these attitudes to her but also had been sexually violated in some way. She literally could not comprehend that sex was clean.

"Maria," I asked. "Is it possible you experienced any sexual molestation when you were a child?"

"Oh no," she answered quickly. "Nothing like that ever happened to me."

"Let me put it a different way," I continued. "Did you have any sexual experiences with any other person when you were a child."

With that question, Maria acted like a treed raccoon. She had a look that said, "Oh my, I think I don't want to be here now."

Finally, with intense nervousness, she tried to answer my question. "I did some bad things with my father," she said. "And with my two older brothers too."

Her story was one of more than ten years of repeated sexual abuse by these family members, and she was carrying the total weight of the guilt for it. Until that moment, she had never known that what she had experienced would be considered molestation.

"Maria," I said, "those things never should have happened to you. They were not your fault. You were molested, Maria. You were taken advantage of by your father and your brothers. No little girl should ever have to go through that."

"But I let them do it," she sobbed. "I shouldn't have let them do it. I shouldn't have done it with them."

We talked for a while, and I gave Maria the name of a good professional counselor who specializes in helping victims of molestation. Our conversation had changed her life. She not only learned that her husband's desire to touch her was not sinful, but she learned for the first time that she was a victim of molestation. She had heard the term before, but it had never been applied to her.

One reason victims in this second category don't realize they are victims is because they misunderstand what constitutes victimization. In Maria's view, a molester is a man who prowls the neighborhood and lures or forces young girls into his van, then rapes them. Tragically, those kinds of crimes do occur, and each of us needs to protect our children and train them how to say no to strangers. Statistically, however, the vast majority of victims of sexual abuse are molested by someone they know and who does not, in the victim's mind, fit the image of a criminal, especially when it is Daddy or a big brother or Mom or Grandpa or Aunt Sally. Another stereotype is that abusers are low income, mentally ill welfare recipients who prey on those like themselves. In reality, the victims and their abusers come from all segments of society, from well-educated, financially secure, and outwardly successful families as well as families from the other end of the spectrum.

When it comes to sexual abuse, much misunderstanding exists about the actual act of molestation. Often people think if sexual intercourse didn't take place, neither did molestation. In reality, molestation can be *any* violation of a person's sexual being, any penetration of that person's sexual space, not just the penetration of the body.

An even greater number of victims of physical and emotional abuse don't know what to call what has happened to them. Once again, the stereotype is of a physical abuser who mercilessly beats a child or who puts a child's hands on a hot burner as punishment or who locks children in closets.

A friend of mine, whom I will call Steve, once told me how he came to realize he had come from a home where emotional and physical abuse had occurred.

Steve and his sister were deeply committed Christians and outstanding musicians. I liked Steve, although he sometimes seemed too committed to his music, too disciplined, if that is possible. He was a hard worker and a good performer, but he never seemed to enjoy what he did.

"After college, I got tired of the way I was living," he told me. "I got weary of music, weary of church, weary of always having to be perfect. I completely fell away from the Lord and went in a different direction, becoming successful in business.

"A time came when my wife told me she was going to leave me if I didn't get help for what she said was my inability to meet her needs emotionally and, more alarmingly, for the way I was treating my children. I didn't realize it at the time, but I was really harming them emotionally. I was distant and demanding. I loved my children and would have died for them, but I was not meeting their needs.

"I finally decided to get counseling. I didn't want a Christian counselor, so I called a therapy center that had been recommended by one of my business associates. As the Lord would have it, I ended up with a Christian, although I did not realize that right away. He also happened to specialize in abuse, and I hadn't known that ahead of time either.

"He immediately zeroed in on my childhood, most of which was a fuzzy memory for me. I knew I resented my father, but I always thought it was because of conflict we had during my teenage years. My resentment turned out to be deeper than that. My father was an angry, demanding, and very rigid man. It was not unusual for us to be spanked with a leather strap for a bad report card or for getting home late from playing with friends. I feared him, and down deep inside I despised him. I also loved him, however, because he was my dad, and there were colorful aspects of his personality.

"Yet Dad seemed always to be upset about something, and sometimes he took that out on us. I remember, for example, once asking Dad to help me build a train set in the garage. We laid out the plans, bought the materials, and started on the construction. He was impatient with me for not knowing the names of certain tools or not moving fast enough when he wanted something. Finally, he got exasperated and lost control of himself and started beating me while at the same time telling me what a dope I was. The whole project was an emotional disaster for me, and I never asked my father to help me with anything like that again."

Steve rarely recalled events like those, and even when he did, he had never acknowledged their destructiveness. After Steve got help, he was able to see his father in a more balanced way, allowing himself to see both the good and the bad about his father. Steve and his father became closer than they had ever been, and because his father had softened over the years, they were also able to talk about some of the hurt.

There was also improvement in Steve's own home. "I understand now," Steve told me, "why I had such a hard time responding to my own children's needs. My childhood was filled with such pain that I didn't feel comfortable entering into their childhood, and I didn't know what to do."

Getting that worked out also helped his relationship with his wife. Steve had enclosed himself in a fortress of protection which had prevented him from freely entering into an intimate relationship with anybody.

THOSE WHO COULD REMEMBER IF PROMPTED BUT HAVEN'T THOUGHT ABOUT IT FOR A WHILE

It's interesting what we choose to remember or to think about and what not to think about. Last year, I spoke at a

Christmas banquet for a large church in southern California. The woman who introduced me had been a friend for
more than twenty-five years. We had attended the same college where we were members of a musical group that spent
an entire summer traveling around the United States representing the school. In her introduction, she recounted a story
from our summer tour about one hot, frustrating day in
Omaha, Nebraska. I was driving our school station wagon
on the occasion she described, and frankly, the traffic and
the streets of Omaha had me totally confused. We were trying to reach a barber shop, and everybody in the car had his
or her own opinion as to which way I should turn, where I
should park, and how I should drive. I finally got sick of the
confusion, stopped the car in the middle of the street, and
announced, "Okay, whoever wants to drive can take over." I
was furious.

The story is obviously not about one of my better moments, and my friend enjoyed poking fun at me. The reason
I'm telling it now is to illustrate how well I remember what
happened that day. I remember which street we were on and
which direction we were traveling. I could probably still find
the barber shop if it were still there. I remember how frustrated and furious I was and how embarrassed I felt later.
What is interesting, however, is that I had not thought about
that painful moment in twenty-five years, until my friend
retold the story. If you had asked me to write a detailed account of that entire summer tour before then, I would have
left that particular story out. I probably had elected not to
think about it again, because it was too painful for me.

I routinely receive letters and telephone calls from people
who say, "I was listening to your program the other day and

when you were talking about victimization, I remembered something like that that happened to me."

One recent call was a classic. I don't remember the caller's name so I'll call him Judd.

"I've been listening for several months now as I drive home each evening from work. As I've heard people talk about incest and molestation, it's always made me very sad. Recently, however, I've begun having brief flashbacks of something like that happening in my family."

"Like what?" I asked.

"At first I didn't know," Judd responded. "It's kind of crazy, but it's as though I just knew something happened. I think I've always had that knowing.

"Then one day, without any warning, I suddenly remembered. I had spent two weeks one summer with a family in another state who lived on a farm. It was a memorable time because of the fun of being in the country, but it was also significant because one of the hired workers at the farm molested me in the barn. I remember it clearly now, and I don't think I had truly forgotten it, but I have not thought about that two-week visit for years."

Many people like Judd can remember if something sparks their memory or if somebody else reminds them, but they have chosen not to think about certain painful events for a long, long time.

THOSE WHO HAVE PARTIALLY OR COMPLETELY BLOCKED THE MEMORY OF WHAT HAPPENED

The fourth kind of victim is the person who seems to have erased whatever happened from memory.

For about five years I have been conducting an informal

poll. Every time I have a guest on my program who is an expert on child abuse or participate in conferences with experts on child abuse, I ask them the same question: "What percentage of the victims of sexual, physical, or emotional abuse do you feel have significantly or completely blocked the memory of it?"

The consistent answer has been, "More than seventy percent."

It would be easy for us to believe that the largest percentage of victims are in the first category, those who remember what happened to them and call it exactly what it is—abuse. The likelihood, however, is that the majority are in the remaining three categories, and especially the last two.

Victims who have experienced blocked memories will sometimes forget whole categories of childhood. Many, for example, can't remember childhood at all. I have talked with numerous people who don't have memories prior to junior high school or high school. Thirteen years of their lives wiped out! Others can't remember anything before the age of five or six, or may remember before and after a particular year or period of years, but nothing in between. Still others may have a whole range of memories from the age of two or three upward but may have eliminated selective subjects like Mom or Dad or Grandma or school or church. A woman I dealt with recently, for example, was molested by her father at the age of four and had no memories of him whatsoever until the age of eight or nine. Others, such as the man described in the first chapter, Dr. Sanderson, have carefully eliminated all bad memories. It is important to point out that even if a person remembers abuse from childhood, it is common that what I call the "branding experience," the particular event that caused the most destruction, is blocked from memory.

A friend named Cheryl is a victim of incest and has always known that. Because she was in touch with those memories and had always been eager for help for her needs, she underwent pastoral counseling, extensive "inner healing," an intense Christian discipleship and personal growth program, and had several years of professional counseling. Though she received valuable help in each case, she knew she had a long way to go and became discouraged. "I just can't stand the thought of beginning the counseling process all over again," she told me. "I have changed through the counseling I've had, but I am tormented still by compulsions and fears that have not been fazed at all."

"You have worked on all this courageously," I told Cheryl, "and in my opinion you have dealt with as much of your past as you are in touch with."

"Then why am I still in torment?" she asked.

"I'm not sure," I replied, "but knowing you as well as I do and how much time and energy you've devoted to getting well, I would guess there is something important about your pain that you have not yet addressed."

"But I remember everything," she responded. "I know what my problem is."

"Nevertheless, I would like to refer you to a friend of mine, a professional counselor who specializes in helping a person uncover a hidden root."

Cheryl started seeing my friend, and over a period of time a startling discovery was made. In grade school, she had been briefly abducted and raped by a stranger at a public campground in the mountains. It had been a horrifying and painful experience, and it had been completely blocked from her memory. The counselor discovered that Cheryl had a deathly fear of campgrounds and would not, under any circumstances, go to one. Eventually she revisited the campground where she was raped to further awaken her memory, after which she began to understand things about herself that never before had made any sense.

REASSIGNING THE FEAR, GUILT, AND ANGER

Even though a person can forget or ignore memories of abuse, the painful effects of that season of destruction do not go away. Fear, guilt, and anger persist. As a result, the pretending victim is faced with a dilemma. He needs to act as though nothing painful happened. He wants to live in a new world where the reality of what happened and what he fears it means about him will not have to be acknowledged. Yet even if the memory is left in the old world, the fear, guilt, and anger are stowaways that come along to the new world. What can the victim do with them? He can't admit what they mean. That would be too painful and would violate his commitment to pretend the past did not happen. So what now? He reassigns them. He attaches the fear, anger, and guilt to things that are in his new world and acts as though the new things are the cause. That is, he practices a new form of pretending.

FEAR

I spoke at a women's retreat once in the mountains of southern California where I was asked to conduct an afternoon workshop on victimization. During that session I talked about the connection between abuse and fear. Afterwards a woman named Laura asked if I could talk with her later. "I'm intrigued with some of what you talked about today," she began when we met to talk. "I have a crazy problem, but something you said prompted me to ask you about it."

"How can I help you?" I asked.

"I'm afraid of spiders," she stated. "What I mean is, I'm really afraid of spiders. I go into hysterics. I hyperventilate. I nearly pass out. All my friends think I'm crazy, and my husband is sick of me. This weekend, I'm not even staying in the cabins at this campground. I'm staying in a motel in a nearby city because I can't stand the thought of spiders. It's a miracle I came to the retreat at all."

"How long have you felt this way?" I asked.

"I have always disliked spiders," she replied, "but my fear has intensified the past four or five years."

"You don't need to apologize for not liking spiders," I said. "I think most folks feel somewhat the same way. But your fear is overwhelming, and you are right that this afternoon's discussion might relate to it. I suspect your fear has actually been caused by something more threatening than spiders, something that would explain the intensity of your fear." Then I asked her, "Did anything we talked about at the workshop relate to you?"

"Yes, but only because I could identify with some of the symptoms you described," she replied. "I don't remember any abuse in my childhood, but then I don't remember much about my early years. I nearly went crazy with emotion while you were speaking, and I have felt sick to my stomach most of the day since then."

Laura mentioned some other problems, such as a repulsion to sex. I told her, "I strongly recommend you see a counselor who specializes in helping victims who block out memories of painful experiences."

A few months later I spoke at Laura's church. She talked with me briefly after the service. "I have been in counseling," she said, "and we've made some startling discoveries."

"Like what?" I asked.

"I was sexually abused," she answered. "My mother was part of a strange group involved in a kind of satanic worship. I found out they used me as part of some of their rituals. That has been terrifying."

"How did you find out?" I asked.

"At first, bits and pieces of memories started coming back during therapy," she replied. "I didn't know whether to trust them. Then I remembered a particular person who was my mother's close friend. I went to visit her and sort of tricked her into admitting some of what went on. I acted as though I remembered it all and talked with her about some of the past. She doesn't believe in the satanic stuff anymore and wishes it had never been part of her life. She told me she often wondered what effect the rituals had on me."

Laura not only came from an emotionally needy home but also had been terrorized. Anyone hearing her complete story would not have faulted her for fearful feelings. Her friends and family would have said, "Laura goes through some moments of fear and panic from time to time because of the awful experiences she had as a child." Because her terror had been transferred to spiders, however, she was considered a "fruit loop" by family and friends. When a person reacts strongly and in a bizarre way to basically harmless aspects of the environment, when a person has exaggerated feelings that don't make sense, we need to recognize this as a possible sign of concealed pain.

I want to issue a word of caution: a person who is afraid of something like spiders is not necessarily a victim. Most of us are afraid of something. Laura's fear, however, was overwhelming and interfered with everyday life. The intensity of her reaction to spiders suggested deep destruction, and her counseling confirmed that.

GUILT

The awful feeling of responsibility for the abuse one has endured and the feeling of being eligible for more pain in life can be reassigned to the most ordinary details of life. Some people experience intense guilt because they didn't get the house cleaned perfectly or they cheated on their diet and ate a piece of cake. This feeling of industrial-strength doom in response to minor failures is often evidence that the guilt has originated elsewhere and has now been reassigned.

ANGER

When it comes to anger, I think most of us have seen what I'm describing. We commonly explain a person's unjust treatment of another person as his "taking it out" on the other person. He is angry about something else but is directing his anger toward somebody who doesn't deserve it. When the root of the anger is early childhood abuse, the result can be powerful.

You may remember a series of shootings on the freeways in southern California. For a few weeks it seemed as though people had gone mad. Dozens of incidents occurred in which motorists pulled guns on one another and blasted away. I interviewed a police psychologist during that time who explained that the perpetrators were people carrying enormous loads of hostility, possibly from childhood abuse.

They redirected that anger toward people who drove too slowly on the freeway or changed lanes without signaling.

Clearly it is important to understand the pretending stage of a season of destruction. At the very least, we elect to live a conscious lie, pretending as though some things about our experiences, our feelings, and our current behavior are not true. At the very most, we block out of memory the branding experience that is so painful to us, and yet without the accompanying ability to conceal the fear, guilt, and anger left as residue.

PART THREE

ENTERING THE SEASON OF RECOVERY

■

CHAPTER 10

TRUTH
The Only Path toward Wholeness

∎

I have officiated at many weddings, each of which has been special in one way or another. One, however, will hold a prominent place in my memories forever. That day, as I stood at the front of the church watching the bride's radiant face and her pure, white gown, I was nearly overcome with emotion. I knew something about her the guests did not know: she had experienced an astonishing season of destruction that began in her earliest years.

I had met Sheila six years earlier when I was asked to write a script for a short film presentation; she was the cinematographer for the project. I was immediately impressed with her intelligence and her competence, but it was obvious she found it awkward to relate to people on a personal level. She also had the uniqueness of always being dressed in soldier's fatigues.

Over time Sheila and I worked on other projects and became good friends. One morning, as we were going over a script, she blurted out, "I was molested when I was a child."

I was momentarily surprised by what she said and how

abruptly she had said it, but I realized this was her way of trying to communicate something deep and important. She had probably spent weeks trying to build up courage to express herself.

"I am very concerned about victimization," I replied.

"I know," she said, "I have listened to you talk about it on the radio."

That was all Sheila wanted to say on the subject then, but in weeks to come, she unexpectedly punctuated our conversation with comments about her molestation. I learned she had been molested for longer than ten years by her father; then she was raped and terrorized by a man who found her sitting alone one evening in a public park. I also learned that although she was trying to live as a committed Christian, her private life was one of fear, sexual compulsions, suicidal thoughts, anger, and guilt.

Even though she was a competent professional, she clearly was haunted by feelings of inadequacy. She had few close friends, and I had never known her to date or have a boyfriend.

"You need to get help for this," I told her. "You are an intelligent, highly motivated person with a lot of life ahead of you. You deserve to know what it is like to live without all this pain."

Sheila was cautious and didn't want to rush into anything, but finally one day she admitted to me, "I have begun to see a counselor."

I don't know when I have ever seen so much growth in a person. Sheila timidly started experimenting with different styles of clothes and wearing light make-up, evidence that she was putting fresh thought into her appearance and that her view of herself was changing. She became increasingly involved in the lives of those around her. Her spiritual life grew. Then one day I received a telephone call from her. "Could I bring a friend to meet you?" she asked.

Later that afternoon, I watched from my window as a car stopped in front of my house. The driver went to Sheila's side of the car and opened the door for her, and they walked hand-in-hand toward my front door. *Good grief,* I thought. *She's got a boyfriend!* Sheila happily introduced me to Ben, a veteran motion picture sound technician she had known for several years. They allowed their relationship to grow in a deliberate and healthy way, and by the time they got married, they had put more effort into making sure it was the right step for both of them than I had ever seen.

One important reason for Sheila's successful recovery was that she had come to a point in her life where she was willing to walk courageously in the direction of her pain. She later told me, "The most significant moments in my recovery were those when I was faced with something scary to do, and I did it." Accepting the first date with Ben, she said, was one of those moments. Another was when she first admitted to me that she had been a victim.

When I think of the word *recovery,* I see a broken, bruised, and shattered girl transformed into a loved and loving woman. Sheila's white wedding dress celebrated the healing that had occurred in her life.

Did the dress and the wedding mean Sheila had become perfect? No. Did they mean she never experienced fear, guilt, or a temptation for compulsive behavior again? No. Did they mean she had arrived in a world where the pain of the past was forgotten and the experiences of the present and future were pure bliss? No. Did they mean she was finished dealing with the pain that had occurred at the foundation of her life? No.

Her wedding did mean, however, that she was no longer hindered or imprisoned by what had happened to her. Some of her problems had vanished. Others remained, but their intensity was reduced. In reality, she had taken a step toward being normal, an important point when it comes to the recovery process. The goal is not to enter a perfect world where no pain exists. That world would not be real. It would be a pretend world. The goal is to live in the real world, where confusing and painful events occur, without being permanently crippled and overwhelmed by them. The real world contains both bad and good, and each of us needs to rely on God for some explanation as to why that is the case and how we can live in the most fulfilled way.

There is hope. Hope for recovery. Hope for wholeness. Hope that the open wounds will heal and only the scars will be left.

I want to summarize what I believe will be important in your season of recovery. I will not emphasize particular techniques because techniques are many and vary from place to place and time to time. Techniques need to be chosen and used wisely, but they are not as important as the goals they attempt to reach. By keeping your eyes on the goals of recovery, you will be better able to find healing.

THE PATH TOWARD WHOLENESS

As you begin your journey of recovery, in which direction should you travel? Where do you go?

Just as your pain occurred during a season of your life,

recovery will take a season as well. No one can predict how long that season will be or prescribe the particular formula to follow. Each person has had unique experiences; the pathway of recovery will be just as unique. However, as a flower reaches for sunlight and a bird flies south for winter, I believe there is a direction you can take with the confidence you are going the right way. That direction is *the quest for truth*.

As you travel toward recovery, you must learn to value truth above all else—to cherish discovering it, knowing it, and making decisions based on it. Until now, you have been dedicated to avoiding pain at all cost. If you were headed toward pain, you automatically chose a different course, regardless of whether or not the new direction was one of health. Our instinct to avoid pain is good, and I'm not advocating we adopt a principle that says, "Experience pain at all cost because if it's painful, it's beautiful." God has given us pain as a sign that something is wrong and needs correction. If I want to solve my problem, I frequently have to walk in the direction of the pain, not because I like pain but because I want to know the truth, which happens to be somewhere in the direction of the pain.

If you have a pain in your side, for example, you know something is wrong. It may be serious, it may not be. If the pain continues or gets worse, you need to see a doctor. That decision can lead to more pain because the doctor is probably going to press on your side to find out what is causing the pain. If the doctor concludes that the cause of your pain is serious and requires surgery, you are again faced with walking toward the pain and even adding the pain that comes with the probing and cutting of surgery. In spite of your pain and the prospect of more pain, you would move toward it because you know that after the operation all the pain would gradually diminish. You would have to experience pain in order to get over your pain.

If you were the kind of person who says, "I'm not going to hurt under any circumstances," you would have avoided seeing the doctor, you would have refused surgery, and ironically, you would have continued in pain, even though your goal was to avoid pain.

Pain can be constructive. Different people going through the same kind of pain do not always experience the same results. Some are destroyed by the experience. Others are strengthened by it. In fact, many people feel their pain has actually launched them into greater heights of success and happiness. The pain of learning that you are not a good baseball pitcher might tempt you to quit playing, for instance, but you would not become a better pitcher without that knowledge. The pain of being told that something in your life needs to change is not pleasant, but it is the prerequisite for being able to change it. It is painful, but it is also truthful.

This pursuit of truth is the theme of the eligibility stage: "What does this mean about me? What truth about myself and the world around me has this helped me to learn?" In reality, an abused child is the innocent victim of a person who has overpowered and hurt that child. You or I would not look at a five-year-old who has been sexually molested and think, *What a slut! How could she do such a thing?* The child, however, thinks about herself in the same way we see the person who abused her. She assumes the guilt and responsibility and thinks, *I am going to interpret every painful event in my life, no matter how small, as a result of who I am and a reminder of it.*

This perspective was described effectively by a man I will

call Chuck, who shared some of his feelings at a conference at which I spoke.

"My family always described me as 'touchy,'" Chuck said. "Almost anything could set me off and make me lash out at my wife and children. One night I beat my wife because she had forgotten to iron my clothes for the next day.

"I realize now that the reason I reacted that way was because of the pitiful way I felt about myself. I felt as if I was the premiere loser of the world. That night, when I walked into my bedroom and realized my clothes were not ironed and ready, I interpreted it as a reminder of what a loser I was. Even my wife was treating me as a loser. I know it sounds bizarre, but that's how I felt.

"There was no such thing in my life as a little failure or a little loss. Everything was a big loss because of how I felt about myself. If my children didn't immediately do what I told them, an angry feeling rose up within me that said, *Don't ignore me. Don't treat me like a loser too.* I would frequently beat them for the smallest things. If I got a ticket from a police officer, even if I knew it was my fault, I'd hear a voice screaming in my head, *You're a loser.*"

Chuck wasn't a loser, of course; he was a person who had the same eligibility to pursue a successful pathway for his life as anyone else—and the same eligibility for experiencing failure, loss, or accident as anybody else. But he had been severely physically abused as a child, and every time his father beat him, Chuck experienced the inner accusation, *You're a loser! You wouldn't be treated this way if you weren't.* A part of him resisted that message and wished it were not true. But another part of him believed it because if it weren't true, why was his father beating him?

TWO IMPORTANT CATEGORIES OF TRUTH

As I have surveyed many hurting people and talked with those who help them, it has become clear to me that the season of destruction attacks two important areas of truth. The season of recovery, then, involves learning the truth about those two categories: (1) the truth about me, and (2) the truth about God.

THE TRUTH ABOUT ME

A significant amount of your pain is the result of believing things about yourself that are not true. As you go through your season of recovery, you will need to gain a truer picture of yourself, your family, and your experiences. Recovery will be a courageous journey to document the real world rather than the world you have constructed in your mind. It's as though a history book is in each of us. Our goal is to make sure this history book is written as accurately as possible. We also want this history book to be complete, without huge gaps which are the result of painful, real experiences that have had a powerful impact on the way we feel about ourselves. I will talk about how we can do this in chapter 11, "Ending the Pretending," and in chapter 12, "Facts and Feelings."

Self-Esteem

If you asked professional and lay counselors, "What is the most common symptom of victimization?" they would probably say, "Low self-esteem." Victims do not have a truthful opinion of their worth or that of others. Some victims hate themselves and are actually self-destructive. Anyone who has worked with victims or has a friend who hurts deeply will see clear evidence of low self-esteem. It sticks out like a giant red badge that says, "I hate me."

One of the movements that has become popular to help overcome this very apparent problem is the "self-love" movement. Nobody can calculate the number of books written, the number of seminars presented, or the number of lectures given in an effort to help people love themselves again. I am not overly critical of the self-love enthusiasts because I think they have launched a sincere effort to help hurting people feel better about themselves. Some of their techniques even work for a short time; but for many people, the commitment to chanting positive phrases or forcing themselves to feel something about themselves that seems contrary to their lifelong identity has consumed an enormous amount of energy and, in the long run, has not worked. The self-love phase of a person's life often has been only a fad and, for many, just another form of pretending.

The goal, I believe, should not be one of self-love but of an accurate self-image. The need is not one of loving myself so much as seeing myself more accurately than ever before.

Victims consider themselves to be cursed and hopeless losers. It is as though there is a nuclear generating plant deep within them that is aglow with the message: "You are a pile of manure." It isn't ultimately very successful for a person in those circumstances to memorize positive slogans or to devote the energy it takes to ignore what he truly and deeply believes about himself. Instead of pasting pretty words on the outside, the victim needs to address what is on the inside. That person needs to come to a place in life where he can say, "I'm not a pile of manure after all. I went through some powerfully harmful experiences that made me think I was, but now I see myself more clearly." Even then, the issue is not one of loving himself but of having a right and real view of himself.

Further, I don't think the deepest hunger of the human heart is to have love for one's self. Rather, it is to be loved. My goal is not to sit in a room or on a hillside and tell myself how much I love myself. My goal is to mean something to the people who mean the most to me. My hunger is to have somebody big and powerful and important in my life say, "I love you," and then I will have the confidence that I am loved. When that big and important and powerful person hurts me and humiliates me and beats me down, it creates the deepest and the most excruciating pain I can ever experience.

THE TRUTH ABOUT GOD

I have never talked with a deeply hurting person who was not struggling with issues about God. Some love God but do not feel they know him. Others feel they are permanently ineligible for any good things from God. Many have deep anger and resentment toward God for what has happened to them. Some are committed atheists because there doesn't seem to be much reason to believe in God when so much pain and destruction has occurred. I tend to believe that many people who are the most militant in their opposition to God feel the deepest hurts from their past.

If you are not a religious person, I don't want the spiritual content of this book to seem like religious propaganda. I am not representing any particular religious institutions, and I don't run an organization for you to send money to. It is my strong conviction, however, that each of us is essentially a spiritual being, and that we have been created by God with an instinctive hunger for a relationship with him.

Many people have taken significant steps in the direction of knowing the truth about themselves, but their efforts have been inadequate because they have not pursued the truth about God. Many nonreligious counselors completely avoid spiritual issues in the lives of their clients and do not realize the extent to which a hurting person is wrestling with this important part of their pain.

On the other hand, we have the fascinating phenomenon of committed religious people, dedicated to learning the truth about God and communicating that truth to others, who live with continual torment because they are out of touch with the truth about themselves. Some of the most deeply hurting people I know are ministers, missionaries, and other full-time Christian workers who outwardly live an upright life but are inwardly buffeted by fear, anger, guilt, and compulsive behaviors. To make matters worse, most of them believe that all they need to do to solve their problems is to have more faith or perform some particular ritual to get rid of their torment. Or they are told that if they were serious about their faith, they would not have any torment at all. But the reality is that for them, the path toward freedom will mean getting in touch with the truth about themselves so the truth they know about God can take effect.

It saddens me that there are churches and Christians who emphasize guilt and condemnation and who, as a result, actually victimize people in the process. I recently interviewed a non-Christian researcher who studied women who had had abortions and how that experience had affected them in later life. He either surveyed or extensively interviewed several hundred women, making several interesting discoveries. One was that the overwhelming majority of these women felt at the time of the abortion that what they were doing was wrong, and they ultimately experienced severe pain and remorse.

I asked, "What helped them recover?"

He listed several contributions to recovery, including "having assurance of God's forgiveness."

I asked, "What about those who were not Christians or who did not approach their healing from a religious viewpoint?"

He paused for a moment and then said, "I haven't interviewed anyone who has truly overcome her pain without seeking God's forgiveness, and most of those have found it through Christianity."

In my experience, the people who have found the deepest and most lasting recovery from victimization (even some who assume that their condition is irreversible like homosexuals) have gone through a season during which the love and message of Jesus Christ has penetrated their darkness.

HOMOSEXUALS

The rising visibility of homosexuality has had the dual impact of causing alarm among the nonhomosexual population and increasing political activism among homosexuals. People who previously kept their homosexual preference a guarded secret are now encouraged to "come out of the closet" and to campaign for homosexuality to be accepted as an alternative lifestyle. Critics say homosexuality is the perverse choice of the individuals involved. Homosexual activists say that their sexual orientation is innate, and there is nothing they can do about it. This is a controversy in which an understanding of victimization plays a key role.

Homosexuals are not all exactly the same, and not every

homosexual has traveled the same path toward his lifestyle. Some persons have become involved in homosexual behavior because they wanted to experiment with every kind of sexual activity they could. Others have felt driven to homosexual relationships because they have felt too much pain in heterosexual involvements. At the core of the homosexual population, however, are those who say they have felt attracted to the same sex since they were children, and even if they want to change that, they feel powerless to do so.

The clear consensus of the professionals I have interviewed, both on and off the air, is that an enormous number of homosexuals are victims of childhood abuse and especially sexual abuse. Theirs is a disorder of sexual confusion rooted in the destruction of "who I am." They feel ineligible to be a "man" or a "woman," or their self-hatred is so pronounced that the original self is repudiated and a pretend self is created, usually with an identity that is as distant from the original identity as possible.

Brian, an acquaintance of mine, lived his life not only as a homosexual but also took the initial steps toward becoming a transsexual, a person who changes his sex through surgery and hormone treatment.

"I felt as if I were a woman trapped in a man's body," he told me. "There was never a time when I wasn't attracted to males. When I went to the movies as a boy, all my friends commented on the beautiful women on the screen, while I was paying attention to the men.

"Like many homosexuals, I felt guilty about what was going on inside me and hungered to be 'normal.' I tried dating in high school and even experimented with heterosexual sex, but just couldn't get interested. I began having homosexual relationships during my last year of high school.

Soon every major decision I made in life was measured by how it was going to affect my homosexual relationships and activities.

"I had always believed in God and would talk to him often when I was in elementary school. I came to feel he was disappointed in me because of my homosexuality, so I didn't feel very close to him when I entered junior high school. Later, as an adult, I attended a few churches but never felt comfortable at any of them. Eventually I became part of a church who welcomed homosexuals and taught there was nothing wrong with it. Even though at the time I claimed to be happy and fulfilled in letting myself 'be me,' I was in torment. Deep inside I knew my life wasn't right.

"The turning point came when a man with whom I worked, and who had always shown me love even though he knew I was homosexual, shared the love of God with me in a way I had never before understood. Christ's love and forgiveness became mine for the first time, and I was nearly intoxicated with it. I knew I had to try to live for the Lord the best I could and that I would have to give up my homosexual behavior. God led me to a ministry for homosexuals that was run by ex-homosexuals. For the first time, I met a group of people who claimed they were no longer homosexual, something I had always been told was impossible to achieve. They loved me, accepted me, and guided me. One key to my success was the realization that I had been a victim of molestation early in life. That experience had literally destroyed me. I spent almost three years in therapy getting in touch with my victimization and what it meant to my life. The result was freedom and understanding."

Brian is now married, has two children, and is involved in ministry to others who are struggling with homosexuality.

For many people an encounter with God has been a critical part of their season of recovery. Many victims, for example, have been invited to what has come to be known as "12-Step Programs," the most famous of which is Alcoholics Anonymous. Other 12-step programs exist for almost any kind of past pain or compulsive behavior. Some people visit a meeting because they have heard of someone else's successful experience, and a few of those visitors are disappointed when they realize so many of the twelve steps have to do with God. They may reluctantly go ahead and become involved in the program but without taking the "God stuff" seriously. Inevitably, however, they do need to take the "God stuff" seriously. That, in fact, is going to be the path toward healing.

The 12-step programs have had a significant impact on the lives of hurting people and may have become the fastest-growing spiritual movement in the nation. As important as it is to place one's trust in a higher power, though, I don't think doing so will be a valid experience unless one is specific about who that higher power is and, more specifically, is trusting in Jesus Christ. Multitudes of victims have entered into recovery from pain through the doorway of Christianity. The reason, I believe, is that who Christ is and what he has done and why he did it is a story of love. It is also a story of people who have been separated from God because of the spoilage caused by sin in the world and the story of a Savior who came to bridge that separation.

Many victims either are so mad at God for what happened to them or have been reared in such religiously unhealthy environments that it has been a long time since anything spiritual has been of interest to them.

Let me say that what happens between an individual and

God is intimate and personal, not institutional. Jesus said that he and the Father love us and reach out to us in love. If we finally receive that love, we will want to do what he asks, and he will actually make his home within us. That is why Christ's message is so life-changing. Even without the experience of victimization, we all experience separation from God and a consciousness of wrong. Jesus died for us to pay for the wrong and to bring us back into a right relationship with God. The cleansing from guilt and the confidence of being loved that comes from this relationship is real and life-changing, the beginning of a lifelong spiritual journey.

Finally, the victim who accepts Christ truly knows and understands God's love for him or her. Now that giant red badge changes from "I hate me" to "God loves me." The victim is free to be who he or she truly is and to be delightfully real with God and with others. This is a quality of "childlikeness."

THE IMPORTANCE OF CHILDLIKENESS

Truth and the feelings in response to truth are part of a childlike world. For this reason some of us have difficulty finding that world. We try to maintain an image of "toughness" and "maturity" and are actually embarrassed by people who have the ability to be childlike in their belief and their emotions.

I am not talking about childishness. To be childish is to act selfishly and destructively. Childlikeness is the quality of being delightfully real with myself, with God, and when possible, with others. If we are honest with ourselves, the emotions deep within us are childlike ones. It hurts when you experience disappointment or separation from someone you love. It hurts when you've been fired from a job or have been slighted by a friend. It hurts when circumstances seem to be going against you. If most of us were honest with ourselves at times like those, we would acknowledge the childlike response of wanting to curl up into a ball and cry. The same is true of enjoyment and happiness. The best times are ones experienced with childlike delight. Many of us do not acknowledge those childlike realities and do not express them or, when appropriate, enjoy them. I don't mean to suggest that everything we feel should be expressed at the time we feel it. That would be childish and harmful. In most daily relationships, we need to be mature and act like adults and to have the wisdom to know what to say and how to say it. There need to be settings, however, when we allow ourselves the privilege of being childlike about our pain and our delights because that is who we are.

Jesus taught that "unless you . . . become as little children, you will by no means enter the kingdom of heaven."[1] What did he mean? Was he advocating childishness? No! He was emphasizing the truth that, in a childlike way, each of us needs to confess our need for him, accept the truth about him, and walk with him in that honest, childlike way. Childlikeness is really wholeheartedness. That's what I think of when I think of children. They trust wholeheartedly. They have fun wholeheartedly. They get angry wholeheartedly. They hurt wholeheartedly. One of the tragic effects of victimization is to fragment that childlike wholeheartedness. The ability to trust, to feel, to have fun, and to grieve in a wholehearted way is injured. That leaves the victim in a state where he can "sort of" trust, "sort of" have fun, or "sort of" be honest about pain.

Getting in touch with truth is to become childlike—

childlike about your emotions, childlike about your anger or disappointments, childlike about the people and the experiences of your life, childlike in your reaching out for help and crying out to God. As you talk, write, and pray, you must give yourself permission to be as childlike as possible because it is in that way you will discover the truth deep inside you, it is in that way you will embrace the truth about yourself and the truth about God.

CHAPTER 11

ENDING THE PRETENDING
Take Another Look at Your Past and Present

■

Pretending is actually a form of shock. For example, if you received news right now that a member of your family was killed in an accident, you would probably go into shock. That's your mind's way of saying, "I can't handle this all at once, so I'm going to shut down some of my systems and gently travel into another world for a while so I can survive." That's why some people seem so calm after a tragedy. They have not fully felt the impact of what happened, but they will in time.

Then there is a season of slowly coming out of your shock, gradually moving back into the real world. That season consists of getting increasingly in touch with the pain and the significance of that pain. Piece by piece the reality of what happened rests upon you. Week by week you are both hurting and healing until at last your recovery is complete, and you have worked through the grief and loss. Finally, there is a day when you can say that even though you will never forget what happened and the emotions of it will never be far from your heart, you will no longer be hindered by it or prevented from living your life and having relationships and accomplishing goals.

To journey toward truth and recovery, you must determine to end any pretending in your life, either about the past or about the present.

PRETENDING ABOUT THE PAST

Part of pretending deals with the victim's history of what happened, especially the history of what was most painful. Sometimes we rewrite the history of our past when reselling it to other people; we construct a story about the way we wish life had been instead of the way it really was. But now is the time to be honest with ourselves.

I have told stories in this book about people who recovered important memories in a short time, sometimes in a single day or evening. That happens from time to time, but for the vast majority of people, the process is a step-by-step one. A professional counselor, Kathleen Case of California, likens it to peeling an onion layer by layer. For most people, that takes time.

REPRESSED TRAUMA

Some people tell me, "I suspect that something destructive happened in my early life, but I cannot remember anything."

I advise these people to find a counselor who specializes in cases of "repressed trauma." Yet many victims have the feeling, "I'd rather do it myself."

When left to our own devices, most of us either fail to see all we need to see or are not able to overcome the intensity of the denial that has kept the truth hidden for a lifetime. Remember that for most victims their energy, intelligence, and talents have been dedicated to keeping secrets by denying the truth.

How do you know whether you have hidden memories of victimization? One clue is identification. If you have identified with the descriptions of victims in this book and/or have experienced the effects of the season of destruction but you can't really pinpoint the root cause, you may be suffering from repressed trauma.

One of the most dramatic stories of repressed memories from victimization I have ever heard is from author, speaker, and counselor Marilyn Murray—an attractive, energetic, and refreshing person who, until the age of forty-four, spent much of her life living in the fast lane. "I was determined to be the most accomplished and Christian woman in town," Marilyn told me. "I played the piano at church, held several Bible studies in my home, and had become the best known woman dealer of western art in the country."

Marilyn was living in Scottsdale, Arizona, at the time, which had given her relief from the severe bouts of asthma that she had experienced as a child in Kansas. Over the years, however, another physical problem had appeared, a pain that she tried to hide from her friends and business associates. I asked Marilyn to be more specific about this pain.

"Severe, blinding, excruciating pain. Mostly in my head but sometimes in other areas of my body as well. It got so bad that I actually considered committing suicide, and I had never been a suicidal person. I got a lot of medical attention and took whatever medications were prescribed, but nothing did the trick, and I felt helpless."

"What finally led you in the right direction?" I asked.

"It was what I have referred to as a 'roast Marilyn' party thrown by some of my closest friends. They had watched me go through the pain, and they knew that I had gotten to the point where I would sometimes literally crawl from my bed to my closet and plead with God to relieve me of my pain. One of them asked me, 'Marilyn, how much pain medication are you taking?' She was jolted when she heard me say, 'Twenty-five Excedrin per day, 125 milligrams of Elavil per day, about 10 to 12 Alka-Seltzer per day, and a bottle of Fiorinal each week.'

"This woman was one of my best friends and was not shy about saying what she was feeling. She gave me a lecture about my condition, and one of her recommendations was that I should get counseling from a clinic in California. She even made arrangements for me to go there, bought the plane ticket, and drove me to the airport. I had tried everything else and couldn't offer a good argument, but I knew that the people there specialized in diagnosing and treating repressed childhood trauma. I protested all the way to the airport that mine had been a perfect childhood."

Most of the patients who went to the California clinic remained there for three or four weeks. Marilyn went with the expectation of being there for only a week or two, then returning home to her family, church activities, and business. For her, however, the stay would be more than seven months and would be the most remarkable case in the history of the clinic.

"I wasn't very cooperative at first," Marilyn told me. "I was interested in finding a way to deal with my pain, but I wasn't convinced that my childhood had anything to do with it. There were a lot of little things that did affect me, however. For instance, when I arrived at the clinic, the weather was cold; that and the older homes in the neighborhood reminded me of my Kansas childhood. That gave me a shiver that went a lot deeper than just my body temperature. Then, on the tenth day of my stay, some feelings and insights and experiences in therapy contributed to what I have called my 'volcano.' A scream that had been buried within me for thirty-six years came to the surface. That was followed by a terrified child's voice that cried, 'I'm only eight! Please, please, I'm so little! Oh, dear God, please don't let this happen to me!'

"Over the next several weeks I regained the memories of what happened, where it happened, and when it happened.

"I was gang raped at the age of eight by a group of soldiers who jumped me while I walked alone to a youth choir rehearsal at my church. They finally knocked me unconscious and left me for dead. The event was so painful and so devastating that it was burned from my conscious mind."

Through therapy, the majority of Marilyn's physical problems disappeared. Her therapist even urged Marilyn to continue her education. She earned both a B.A. and an M.A. degree in psychology and entered into a Ph.D. program—all in forty-four months. During this time, Marilyn developed a theory of the psychological splitting process that happens in the life of the victim of repressed trauma, which she calls "The Scindo Syndrome." I believe that theoretical models like hers could contribute to a new view of theories of personality. She conducts seminars for psychological and medical professionals and for sex offenders in Arizona prisons, and she is probably the only rape victim who is going into prisons to help rapists recover from the hurts of the past.

PRETENDING ABOUT THE PRESENT

Charlie is the prototypical "macho man." He has jet black hair and a body finely honed through hours spent at a health club. He wears generous amounts of gold around his neck, arms, and fingers. He is rich, good-looking, and tough, and he knows it. He is also one of the great pretenders.

Charlie's wife, Wendy, has been trying for years to deal with some serious problems in Charlie's life. One of the biggest is that it is impossible to criticize Charlie to his face. It doesn't matter whether the criticism is big or small, he will fly into a rage. Sometimes that includes beating his wife or children, sometimes he stomps out the door and disappears for a few days. "Being wrong" makes him feel so sensitive that he cannot handle it.

A lot of folks hate a person like Charlie because they think he realizes what he is doing. The fact is, Charlie does not see things the way they really are. To us in the real world, he seems unreasonable, abusive, and childish. In Charlie's pretend world, however, he is the charming prince who can do no wrong. Anyone who tries to convince him otherwise is, in his view, a person with serious problems of his or her own and a threat to his existence. He thinks his wife is a lazy, complaining, and negative person who does not appreciate his finer qualities. He views his children as unmotivated and untalented and never misses a chance to tell them so, thinking that will shame them into doing better. From Charlie's standpoint, he is a fine father and a loving husband who provides unselfishly for a family who is ungrateful. He views them as a curse.

As you try to be honest with yourself, you discover "pretendings" you were unaware of before. You pretend to be better than you are in some respects and worse in others. You can arrange your pretend world in any way that seems to serve your purposes.

FORGETTING THE PAST?

"Why do I have to spend so much time dealing with the past?" I am asked frequently. "I thought the Bible says we are to forget 'those things which are behind' and to 'press toward the goal for the prize of the upward call of God in Christ Jesus'?"[1] I think the apostle Paul would be irritated if he knew people were using his words to encourage others to leave unfinished business in their lives. Paul was not arguing against dealing with the past. He was saying we should not be held back by the past, we should not be immobilized and paralyzed by what has already happened.

Let's imagine a certain pastor is concerned for a man in his church. The man is a committed Christian and a leader in the church. The man has confessed to the pastor, however, that he struggles with a lot of depression and fear and is in bondage to compulsive behaviors. The pastor is discouraged because he has tried to help the man, but with no lasting success.

One day the pastor learns that twenty years earlier this man had robbed a bank, killed two bank guards, had been arrested and convicted, sentenced to prison, and had later broken out of prison and moved to a part of the country where he could establish a new identity and a new life. The man had been a criminal in hiding all these years and had pretended with his family and friends that all those things had never happened. Inside, however, he was tormented with guilt and the fear of being found out and apprehended.

He had never allowed the Word of God, the prayers, counsel, and advice of his pastor, and the comfort of his family to be applied to that huge, hurting, and deeply important part of his life.

If you were that pastor, what would you do? Would you pat him on the head and say, "Don't worry about it. We're not supposed to pay any attention to the past. Just forget we ever talked about it, and grit your teeth and face the future"? I don't think so. You would probably say, "No wonder you've been in such pain. There's a lot of unfinished business here. You need to make this right between you and the law, between you and God, and between you and your family. You need to confess to your wife that you have deceived her all these years. She needs to know the truth. You need to contact the authorities and say, 'Here I am. Let's do what is right, even if it is painful.' You need to resolve all this so you can get on with your life. In an ironic way, going back to prison may set you free!"

Large numbers of victims are living lives identical to that man's because they truly believe what happened is due to their own badness, their own criminal credentials. The Bible reads, "He who covers his sins will not prosper"[2] and until victims understand otherwise, that is exactly what they are doing—hiding what they think is their sin. How can there be prosperity in that life? How can we say to that person, "It is unscriptural to deal with the past" and leave him or her with the torment? Dealing with victimization is no mystery. It is not psychological hocus pocus. It is learning what is true about you, what is true about God, and applying the truth about God to the truth about you. "And you shall know the truth, and the truth shall make you free."[3]

CHAPTER 12

FACTS AND FEELINGS
Uncover Hidden Areas of Your Life

■

Think for a moment about what a massive storehouse of information you are. Everything you have ever experienced or felt, thought or learned has been filed away in your brain somewhere. The brain, much like a computer, accepts enormous amounts of data and does amazing things with it. Feelings, however, involve more than just the brain. Emotions can cause butterflies or knots in the stomach, numbness in the extremities, lightheadedness, throbbing, fainting, and a whole host of other reactions. In other words, information involves facts, but feelings involve passion.

It is of monumental importance that both feelings and facts percolate to the surface during one's season of recovery. It does not matter whether the facts and feelings are bad or good, hurtful or healing, they need to be expressed. In fact, I would argue that some of what is felt deep inside us actually takes on a different and more complete form when it is expressed.

One common characteristic of deeply hurting people is their inability to express emotion. Feelings somehow have gotten short-circuited, a kind of emotional constipation.

Hundreds, maybe thousands, of feelings have never been expressed or, at least, not expressed based on the truth associated with those feelings. Emotions just sit there fermenting, causing all kinds of emotional gas pains. For some people, the whole realm of expression seems foreign. Not only have they not cried or talked out their feelings, but musical or artistic expression has not been part of their experience either. Others can be expressive in some ways, while hiding facts and feelings that have never been adequately expressed.

This is especially true when it comes to anger. Some victims have been reared in homes where expression of anything negative was strictly forbidden. Others have come to realize that the intensity of their anger is so great that it is a risk to ever allow any of it to be expressed. And there are those, especially Christians, who feel guilty about anger.

During the season of recovery, it will be important to develop some healthy ways to express your anger, whether that be beating the wall with a pillow or walking in the forest where you can let it out. Even if your anger is inappropriate or out of proportion, it doesn't do any good to pretend as though it is not there. The first step toward making something right is to be honest about what is wrong.

As you journey into recovery, expression should become an intimate friend. There should be nothing of any emotional significance you have not expressed in some way. That will include facts and feelings of the past as well as the present, even those we would be tempted to think are insignificant or unimportant.

THE IMPORTANCE OF JOURNALING

One helpful tool for the season of recovery is a journal. A journal need not be a "dear diary" project, although it can be. A journal is simply a written record of anything you consider important enough to write down. Some people write in their journals once a week or twice a month. Others write in their journals several times a day. There is no limit to how often or how much you write. The importance is that you start writing important details of the past or present that relate to your desire to recover.

The type of journal is up to individual choice. Some people buy blank books. Some use looseleaf folders. Others use their computers. Still others carry pieces of paper to jot down entries when they are away from home so they can later transfer them to their journal. I know several people who carry micro-cassette recorders in their purses or briefcases for this purpose. Some people organize their journal into various categories and sections; others record information as it occurs to them and don't worry much about trying to organize it.

You can use your journal for keeping any record you wish, but let me suggest some of the categories of information that will be important to a season of recovery.

MEMORIES

Start by constructing a history of your childhood as you remember it. Draw simple floor plans of the houses or churches or schools that were important to your childhood. Try to recall the names of friends, neighbors, or family members and what significance they had (or did not have) in your life. Reflect on how you felt about those around you or how they seemed to feel about you. Pay special attention to what I call the "branding experiences," those events in life that helped you form your opinions of yourself. Pay particular attention to anything that was painful or that seemed to involve loss.

Even though the majority of deeply hurting people are victims of abuse, not all destruction has been caused by abuse. Some people experienced the death of a parent or some other important person early in life or have spent a lifetime trying to overcome the devastation of a learning disability or a serious childhood illness. Still others have been deeply affected by the divorce of parents or from growing up in the home of an alcoholic (which frequently does involve abuse).

FACTS AND OTHER PEOPLE'S MEMORIES

In addition to the memories of childhood, try to assemble facts from other sources. Sometimes when you actually visit your childhood neighborhood or the house your family owned, it turns out to be different from what you remembered.

You might also record the memories and opinions of other people. Sometimes they will confirm what you remember, sometimes they will not. Sometimes their memories will comfort and reassure you. Sometimes the opposite will happen. Other people's memories may help you realize that some of your memories are distorted or embellished.

INSIGHTS

As you think about your life, your pain, and your desire to recover, you will have important revelations along the way. Write those down. For example, you may write, "Today I realized my father didn't hate me as much as I feared," or, "I now see why I have been treating my wife the way I have."

DREAMS

Dreams are an important part of our lives, because they sometimes contain clues about what is happening deep inside. Dreams can be elusive, however; in fact, they can be completely forgotten after you've been awake awhile. Keep pencil and paper by your bedside or a small tape recorder and record simple outlines of your dreams while they are still fresh, even if you must do so in the middle of the night.

CURRENT EVENTS AND FEELINGS

The journal can be a diary of sorts, a record of what is happening day by day in your life, especially as those events relate to your pilgrimage of recovery. But one of the more helpful roles of the journal is the avenue it offers you for reflecting your feelings, feelings of either the past or the present. The process of expressing those feelings is vital, and having a record of your feelings for later reflection and evaluation is priceless.

Try to avoid the temptation of writing something like, "Today I remembered when Grandmother died" when you probably ought to describe in detail how you felt when Grandmother died and how you feel now when you think about it. Sometimes hurting people have found valuable expression by writing a letter to another person about how they are feeling or writing a prayer to God or even a letter to themselves. Even though you will not send the letter to the person who victimized or disappointed you, you can put some of your feelings into expression. Then you can either destroy the letter or file it in your journal.

If you lost someone meaningful to you during childhood, a letter of good-bye to that person or a letter of apology or whatever it is that you are feeling can sometimes be a step of healing. I also encourage people to write their story as though it were a book. That doesn't mean it will be published, but it could be helpful to you and, occasionally, to others with whom you wish to share it. Many victims have experienced a giant step in their recovery as they put their story into writing.

If writing is not a satisfying form of expression for you, don't worry about it. Not everyone can express themselves through writing, and not everyone feels comfortable trying. Some people have learning disabilities that interfere with writing. These people may want to go through the same process by talking into a tape recorder or talking to a friend.

TALKING

Even if writing is easy for you, don't underestimate the importance of talking about your experiences and feelings. It is amazing how little of what some people feel or have felt has ever been expressed out loud. It is also amazing how beneficial talking to someone can be. People often say to me, "I never talked about that before, and now that I have, the problem doesn't seem as big."

A man I will call Ernie was a minister and an effective communicator. The subject of death had always haunted him, as it does many of us. But for him it was overpowering and obsessive. He entered into therapy with a professional counselor, and not surprisingly, he discovered he was a victim who had repressed his victimization.

"One day I went to the counselor," he related to me, "and she asked me to describe in detail what it was about death that particularly bothered me. The first thing that came to my mind was my fear of my father dying and the dread I had always felt of having to view him in a casket. I had decided that when he died, I would not view his body because I didn't want to carry that memory with me."

But despite Ernie's efforts to not let his father's death consume his thoughts, Ernie said he had thought about his father's death, especially at bedtime, three or four times a week for more than twenty years!

"It was very difficult for me to put my fears into words," he continued, "but I did so quite simply and in a very short time. As I heard myself saying the words, I thought, *Here I am actually saying what I have feared so much and thought about so much.* It seemed unreal, and I believed that saying what I felt out loud might somehow make it actually happen. When I finished, however, I sat looking at the counselor, very aware of my emotions, and thought, *Well, you've done it. You've confessed your fear.*

"I guess a part of me expected the world to change. I felt okay, however, and not particularly horrified. It was as though I had just killed a demon, and the counselor and I were sitting there looking at it as it lay on the floor. A couple of nights later I was getting ready for bed, and the old haunting fears threatened to overwhelm me. Suddenly I realized that the thought of my father's death was not a pleasant one, but it all suddenly seemed to be in perspective."

What had happened to Ernie was nothing more complex than transferring one of his lifelong painful feelings from the less-than-real world of his imagination to the real world of verbal expression. The mere act of talking about it diffused the fear. Ernie had a similar experience about two years later when he decided to talk with his family about his own death.

"I had always been horrified by the thought of lying in the grave," he said, "so I decided it would help me emotionally if I told my family I would like to be cremated." A week after he had told his family of his decision, he realized he didn't really care what was done with his body after he died, because he wouldn't be living in it anyway. He had always believed that in his head, but his heart had not agreed.

A woman I will call Greta was in counseling for many months before she actually described what had happened to her. She had been raped when she was in elementary school. "Somewhere inside of me was the firm belief that if I ever were to actually speak of what happened to me, I would die on the spot," she told me. "I'm not sure whether that was the result of a threat from the rapist or a decision I made by myself." Whichever, that kept a very intelligent woman from saying what needed to be said.

"One day I decided I was going to say it," she continued, "and so I very softly said to my counselor, 'I was raped by a man when I was a little girl.' I sat there with my eyes closed and my hands clenched and just knew lightning was going to strike me from heaven. When it didn't, the first thought I had was, *I'm still alive!* It was glorious!" The place that memory had occupied in her heart became a lot smaller after that experience, and her therapy advanced in giant leaps.

Who Would Be a Good Listener?

I suggest you talk to a person who understands your particular kind of pain. If you've lost a parent in death when you were a child, find somebody who also has experienced that but who has recovered. If you are a victim of incest, talk to a recovered victim of incest. If you are the child of an alcoholic, find help from others who know the same pain. If you are being abused right now, get help from those who have a special understanding of abuse.

You may be thinking, *I don't know anyone who has experienced my kind of pain.*

Let me suggest that you look for a support group. Begin with your local telephone directory. Look under key words such as *incest, victims, alcoholism, eating disorders,* or *grief recovery*. Check with churches and other volunteer organizations or hospitals or police departments in your community. You can even call the county offices in your area and ask them to refer you to whatever department handles the particular need you have.

When choosing a professional counselor, it is important to get one who has a special understanding of victimization. The best way to find the right counselor is through referrals from people who have successfully dealt with their own victimization or from organizations that focus on victimization. I also recommend (especially if you are Christian) a Christian counselor, because as I have already pointed out, the pathway toward healing is one of learning the truth about you and the truth about God. Dealing with only one of those pursuits will, in my opinion, be inadequate. If you are going to a counselor who will not deal with you on a spiritual level, find a good church or Christian support group so you can nourish your need to deal with the truth about God.

TEARS

I cannot overemphasize the importance of crying in response to some of the painful feelings you will express during the season of recovery. Some things have never been cried out. Or you may have cried, but without understanding.

During a time when I was dealing with some of my own childhood, the memory of a puppy, a cute little Cocker Spaniel named Skippy, occurred to me as I was driving down the freeway one day. I got Skippy when I was seven years old, and shortly after, my parents decided to visit my grandmother who owned a large southern California orange ranch. While there, Skippy disappeared. I don't know whether he got lost or was stolen or was killed by another animal. My father and grandmother scoured the hills until well after nightfall, but we never saw Skippy again.

As I was driving down the freeway thirty years later, however, a childlike utterance came from my lips. I asked, "Why? How could my puppy just disappear? What could have happened to him? Why don't I have my puppy?" The main cry of my heart was, "I don't understand!" As I reflected on that event, my eyes filled with tears, and I began to cry. The more I cried, the deeper the pain seemed to reach. Finally I had to pull over to let myself sob without becoming a traffic hazard.

I couldn't believe how deeply that incident had affected me. My heart continued to be sensitive about it for several weeks, and I cried about it on two or three occasions. The emotions of that event had never been fully expressed, especially since, as a child, I had hoped each day that Skippy would return. My tears at the time had been tears of hurt and confusion and, perhaps, anger over losing my dog. The tears I shed as an adult were tears of compassion for that little boy who couldn't comprehend what was going on.

You will find that as you allow the tears to flow, you will have similar experiences. The tears will be different from time to time—tears of anger, tears of confusion, tears of horror, tears of guilt, but also tears of understanding, of healing, of innocence.

Southern California psychologist Dr. Mark Johnson once told me about a patient of his who had never cried about her pain. She said, "I think I finally understand why it is so hard for me to shed any tears over this. You see, I still can't believe that it wasn't my fault, and if I were to really let myself cry, it would be admitting my innocence."

She was right. That's exactly why I encourage you to write, talk, and cry about what's bothering you. Tears often wash away the pain.

WHAT DO I DO WITH THE TRUTH?

A common question is, "What do I do with the truth of what I am remembering? Should I confront the people who were involved in hurting me? Should I go to my parents and others in my family and tell them what is going on?"

My answer is, "Probably not yet."

Ultimately, it will be important for you to share the memory, or even the responsibility, for what happened, but the first thing to do is to consult a skilled counselor and to make decisions within that counseling relationship as to what should be communicated to whom and when. Often a person who has finally decided to deal with the pain of victimization wants to announce it to the family or to angrily, or even lovingly, confront whoever perpetrated the victimization.

I recommend waiting. Any communication or confrontation of that sort should come from the depth of your healing, not from the depth of your hurt. Also, many families in which abuse has taken place are skilled at pretending, and they will deny the truth of what has happened or will refuse to do anything to respond to it in a healthy way. Other families often resent that the information was brought into the open. Many family members know that some kind of abuse is occurring in their midst, but their ethic is "Don't make waves." Anyone who decides to deal with the problem may be viewed as a traitor. In fact, professional counselors and researchers who used to focus on the victim of abuse are now talking about the "abusive family" and the entire structure of the home.

The denial of truth can happen in larger settings than just the family, such as in churches, schools, or entire communities. In a recently publicized case in southern California, a junior high school student revealed she had been continuously molested by one of the more popular teachers in the school. The teacher denied it, and massive public support was mobilized on his behalf. Meanwhile the girl was ridiculed, and her motives for making the accusations were questioned. She went through torture for telling the truth. Eventually it was proven the molestations did take place, and the teacher was forced to admit what had happened. Even after that, however, some people in the community thought the girl should have kept her mouth shut and that the teacher should have been reinstated to the classroom.

The reasons for ultimately disclosing the truth are numerous.

1. You are released from your guilt. As you deal with your pain, you eventually will realize that you have privately carried the responsibility and guilt for what happened to you and that you have felt imprisoned and confined by it. To tell whoever needs to know what happened and to let the responsibility for your victimization rest on the perpetrator is a healthy step. I am not talking about taking revenge. I am talking about a decision on your part to live again in the real world, a world where you are the victim and where you need to take responsibility for your own life and future but do not need to carry the weight of guilt for what somebody else did to you.

2. *Sharing your story may help rescue others who are still being hurt or those who are past victims.* Unless something or someone has intervened in the life of an abuser, the abuse may still be going on. When one victim comes out of the closet and tells the secret, others have the courage to follow. Or, the revelation that abuse once occurred helps responsible people realize it may still be happening. Decisions can be made then to protect those who may currently be affected by the abuser.

The pattern of victimization is often a repeated one, and if you can help hold someone accountable for what he or she has done, the chances of future victimization will be reduced. Even in cases where the perpetrator does not receive help, the truth can stop the destructive chain.

3. *Your coming forward will sometimes force the perpetrator to get help.* The abuser not only needs to be halted but also deserves help. You would be surprised how many victimizers are able to deal successfully with their problems and enter into safe relationships once again.

The goal, then, of dealing with the past is to see it as truthfully and accurately as you can. Dealing with the facts helps you separate fact from fiction, and the result is a healthy one.

You may ask, "But won't this make me hate my parents or other family members who I have always pretended were perfect?" My answer is, "Not at all." If you are pretending they are perfect, you are probably hiding resentment and anger toward them anyway. In other words, you may hate them already. Admitting to yourself that you have those feelings will be the first step toward resolving them and eventually building an honest relationship with your family.

Once you have looked honestly at the past and the present, you are ready to clarify the question: Who was responsible for what happened to me?

CHAPTER 13

RESPONSIBILITY
Accept Responsibility for Your Life

■

The issue of responsibility is a troublesome one to the hurting person. On the one hand, victims tend to carry virtually the entire weight of responsibility for what happened to them. On the other, they are often unwilling to accept responsibility in the real world.

One of the goals of the season of recovery is to answer two important questions about the subject of responsibility: (1) Who or what is responsible for what happened to me in the past? (2) Who or what is responsible for what happens now?

WHO IS RESPONSIBLE FOR MY PAIN?

The process of ending the pretending should answer the question: Who was responsible for what happened to me? A victim of incest, for example, should not carry any responsibility for what happened, but, as I have said, most of them do. In addition, they might have felt a close emotional tie to the person with whom the incest occurred or experienced

173

some secret enjoyment of the forbidden sex. Not all molestations are violent ones. Sometimes a victim has been induced into a sexual relationship because of the emotional payoff for him or her. Others feel they could have said no or done something to interrupt the abuse or to report it.

Let me ask you a question. When you hear about an adult who has been caught having sex with a child, do you ever blame the child? I hope not. There is no excuse, no justification for an adult having sex with a child, or for that matter, forcing himself or herself on another adult. No matter what kind of second thoughts a victim might have about what happened, the responsibility has to rest on the person who decided to violate someone else's mind, body, and emotions. That's how the law looks at it, and that's how the victim should look at it.

A child who has lost someone in death, suffered neglect, serious injury, disease, war, or other painful experiences should not feel as if he or she is a pile of manure. Disease and accident occur at some time to everyone on earth, so they cannot be taken as selective comments from the cosmos about a person's worth.

WHO IS RESPONSIBLE FOR WHAT HAPPENS NOW?

One of the biggest factors obscuring the responsibility question, in my opinion, is superstition. The victim often is tempted to think, *Since my pain has always seemed to be there and I have no reasonable explanation for it, I conclude that there is a force in the universe, whether it be God or fate, that is determining my future by the same twists of sorrow that have characterized my past.* Suzanne is an example of what I mean.

SUPERSTITION

I always noticed Suzanne during services on Sunday mornings because she was a large person and wore brightly colored clothes and lots of jewelry. Suzanne's appearance prompted a certain amount of curiosity in me about what kind of person she was. I had the opportunity to find out when she made an appointment to talk.

"I'm worried about how God feels about me," she began. "I have tried to live as I should, but I don't seem to be able to. I think God must surely be tired of me. I've been trying to find a job for more than five months, but nothing is happening and that worries me. I feel God is punishing me."

Further conversation with Suzanne revealed she was very fearful and depressed and was living with an enormous amount of guilt. Not surprisingly, she was a victim of incest.

"I try to read my Bible as much as I can," she told me. "I also try to attend church as often as possible, but I can't always make it because I have to visit my mother in the retirement community where she lives."

"Suzanne," I replied, "it is right and healthy to read the Bible, attend church, and even to visit your aged mother, but it doesn't sound to me as if you are doing those things with a healthy motive."

"I don't understand what you mean," she said.

"What do you think will happen to you if you forget to do one of those things or, for some reason, cannot?"

She thought for a moment, and then said, "I guess I believe God will punish me, that he will be disappointed in me and get me for it."

"How do you know that's how he will respond?"

"I just know it," she answered.

"Suzanne," I asked softly, "have you always felt you are a failure in God's eyes?"

Suzanne pulled out a Kleenex and sat in silence while years of pain started rising to the surface.

"It feels like a curse, doesn't it, Suzanne?" I continued.

She nodded in agreement. "I never have put it into those words, but that's how I have felt," she said. "Does that mean somebody put a curse on my life?"

"Your feeling involves unfinished business related to the incest," I told her. "Multitudes of victims feel exactly the same way: accursed. They live with the belief that something is bad about their lives, something that makes them ineligible for good things to happen. The feeling of badness has a mystical quality. It seems like a curse, and it produces a strong superstition in the life of the person who is experiencing it."

"I'm not superstitious," she quickly answered.

"There is a kind of religious superstition, even a 'Christian' superstition, that I think you are suffering from," I said.

"Like what?" she challenged.

"Like your attitudes about reading the Bible, attending church, and caring for your mother," I replied. "Those actions could be done with healthy motives, but you are doing them superstitiously, with the hope that if you do them, the curse will be disarmed. For you, reading the Bible is a ritual because of your fear of the curse, not because you want to be nourished by what it says. It is as though you are saying to yourself, *If I read the Bible today, I will be blessed and have a good day, but if I don't, I will be cursed and have a bad day.*"

"Now that I think about it," Suzanne admitted, "I have

made superstitious choices my whole life, only I never called them that. I have to confess that a lot of my Bible reading doesn't really do much for me, but I feel guilty if I don't do it. I honestly have feared that the reason God has not given me a job is because I got behind in my Bible reading. I spent most of yesterday trying to make up for it, and I guess I felt that would earn me the 'blessing' of getting a job."

"Isn't it sad," I interjected, "that for you, the Bible has been little different than a lucky horseshoe. It has been a magic charm to deal with curses, not the Word of God to feed and nourish you and help you grow and learn."

"That's really true," Suzanne agreed. She also realized that some of what she was doing for her mother was being fueled by the same motives.

Superstition is the true religion of many victims. Deep within is a profound spiritual sadness, a feeling that "if God exists he has either forgotten about me or never cared for me in the first place. Somehow I have rendered myself ineligible for the good things he does for other people." Like Suzanne, they view other people as being blessed and themselves as being cursed. Every bad thing that happens in the life of the victim, then, becomes a fresh reminder of the accursedness and seems to verify it. The victim does not say to herself or himself, "I am a somewhat normal person who experienced failure." The victim concludes, "I am a failure. There is a curse on my life." The prayer of the victim is not, "Forgive me, Lord, for what I did," but rather, "Forgive me, Lord, for who I am."

This is why "magical thinking" is common among victims. The curse seems to have been magically bestowed so there must be some magical solution to remove it.

Each new friend, each new romantic interest, each new church, each new job, each new place to live is viewed as a potential antidote to the mystical pain and badness. There is a moment of hope: "This might finally mean the curse is broken. This is my magical moment." But even the most normal of lives will keep experiencing pain and loss, so when they eventually happen again, the victim goes into a tailspin of despair and concludes that the curse is not gone after all.

A person in this condition is easily attracted to cults or occultic religion. Their superstition and feelings of ineligibility have made many of them feel cut off from God. They instinctively feel attracted to occultic and cultic environments. In fact, the experience of victimization is very much like being in a cult. A victim has been overpowered by a leader who has enormous influence in the victim's life and frequently requires continuing allegiance and service (such as an abusive parent or spouse does). The abuser will punish the victim if there is any question of disloyalty or if the victim dares to break away from the abuser's power. Often family members will also punish the victim for breaking away. The dynamics of a cult are very similar to the dynamics of an abusive family or abusive relationship. That may be why so many victims feel at home in cultic or unhealthy authority-oriented environments.

The increase in Satan worship and demonic activity occurring now is better understood in the light of victimization. I believe in demonic activity, and I have dealt extensively with those who claim to be affected by demons. Some of these people are not demonized but are suffering from complex and severe psychological conditions for which they need professional help. In the cases where I believe demonization has been a factor, it is important to note that virtually every one has involved a person who is a victim of abuse. The devastation and destruction of the abuse has laid waste that person's life, and severe spiritual complications have resulted. To deal effectively with these cases requires understanding the roots of what has made them vulnerable for demonization and that means dealing with their victimization.

A victim's superstitious approach to life is another reason why they often feel helpless. It is healthy, for example, for a person who realizes the truth of cause and effect to say to himself, *I'm running out of money so I need to find a job*. Or, *I'm not performing well for my employer so I need to ask for help and further instruction so I can become a better employee*. Or, *My marriage is going through some difficulty so I need to think and pray about what steps would make it better and take some of those steps*. In other words, there are solutions to problems.

The victim, however, tends to think, *Well, I'm cursed. That's all there is to it. All this bad stuff is happening because of who I am. I can't really change that, so why try?*

Do you see what kind of a trap that is? Do you see why a lot of people in that condition feel like ending their lives? For them, their existence is the problem, so they feel that to stop existing would save themselves and the world a whole lot of trouble.

To many victims, life is something that "just happens," and they feel powerless to have any influence. They will stand at the threshold of important decisions regarding career or marriage (or even hobbies or personal interests) and find it difficult to make any definitive choices because down deep inside they are resigned to fate, to superstition.

When a person finally wakes up one morning and realizes, *There isn't anything mystical about my failures, and I can take definite steps to solve some of my frustrations,* this person's life completely changes. The jobless person starts seeking help and wisdom about his joblessness. The angry and frustrated wife and mother seeks help about the skills of being a wife and a mother. The otherwise successful person who is tormented with fear, anger, and guilt decides to get the insight of a counselor. That is when an otherwise helpless person realizes that God has placed us in a cause-and-effect world, and that He instructs us to learn how to make reasonable decisions about our lives.

As a victim, your season of recovery, then, will be a time of slowly realizing there is no curse over your head. At the same time, you will realize that you can make choices for your life, and that the responsibility for participating in relationships, succeeding in careers, and making the most of your life rests on your shoulders and nobody else's. You can no longer feel trapped and blame your imprisonment on "forces" outside your control. It won't work anymore to resent your husband or your wife for not being the "blessing" you thought you deserved. You cannot repeatedly blame your bosses and supervisors for your chronic inability to keep a job.

Yes, we all run into bad people along the pathway of life, and, yes, unfair and unjust things happen to us. But that is part of life. The decision about what to do next is ours and ours alone. If we decide to resent and blame God or our spouse or our employer—or anyone or anything else—for our position in life, and thereby coop ourselves up in a limited emotional world, *we* have chosen to do so.

RESPONSIBILITY FOR YOUR BODY

The task of assuming responsibility also involves caring for your own body. Even when victims deal successfully with emotional and spiritual issues, they may still feel the haunting effects of fear, guilt, or anger, or the tendency toward compulsive behaviors, which originates from the effect of their pain upon their bodies.

Many of you have already discovered that if you eat certain foods, become addicted to certain substances, or allow your body to get too much out of shape, this abuse can have a dramatic effect on how you feel. For some people depression can be dramatically treated by getting good food, rest, and exercise. Learning what physiological factors may be involved in your personal struggle with pain can be a significant part of your recovery.

The apostle Paul taught that each of us has a tendency toward evil, a result of the spoiled world in which we live. This tendency is like a genetic disease. Even though each of us wants to be kind to others and to serve God, this presence in our bodies seems dedicated to taking us in the opposite direction. Paul refers to that presence as "the old man" or "the flesh."[1] When a person responds to God's love and becomes a Christian, the "new man" comes to life and offers the hope of being able to overcome the temptations of the old man. That old man is always there, however, and is a source of all kinds of torment.

Paul warns that the flesh can take control, if we allow it, and that when it does, our lives will be severely affected. In fact, at one point he lists the products of the flesh. He mentions immorality, sensuality, idolatry, sorcery, strife, jealousy, outbursts of anger, envying, and drunkenness. Then he goes on to offer the good news that with God's power the strength of the flesh can be broken in the life of the Christian.[2]

Paul seems to say that if any part of the flesh controls us, all physical desires can potentially control us. In other words, if you allow a compulsive behavior like drinking to get out of control, you seem to give permission for all of the effects of the flesh to control you. This is a spiritual perspective on what many people have discovered about themselves physically and nutritionally. Some people, for instance, can change from being normal to being emotional basket cases in a short time, depending on what they eat. Isn't it interesting that when the body is impaired, the result is usually something evil? If you don't get enough rest, for example, your disposition does not improve. You don't get sweeter and more patient.

In the same way, the amount of stress that most victims have lived with for years takes its toll on the body. This stress will make other existing conditions, like premenstrual syndrome, much worse.

If you are not paying attention to the medical, physiological, and nutritional aspects of your life, you may be going through unnecessary pain. Find a good medical or nutritional counselor who can help you identify the foods and other substances that may be affecting you. Experiment with improving your overall physical well-being. Establish a daily exercise routine. For some, such changes can make all the difference in the world.

WHAT ABOUT GOD'S RESPONSIBILITY?

Where is God in all this? Does he have any responsibility? Can't I hold him accountable for the pain I've experienced, and doesn't that mean that he should be the one to make things right in my life?

I'm not going to pretend to know the exact answers to those questions, and I don't want to be guilty of offering slick answers. Still, I will suggest a place for you to begin thinking about these questions. If you view this world as paradise—exactly as God created it—where everything happens by his decree, then you may be upset with him. The teaching of the Bible, however, is that the world we know is not exactly the way God created it. It has been spoiled because of the choices of the people God placed here.

Why did he give people the choice to do wrong? I don't know, but it is abundantly clear that he has given every one of us the freedom to choose as we wish. His gift of free will is authentic. He doesn't say, "You can choose as you wish," and then reach down and say, "No, you can't choose that after all." That would be a cruel game on God's part.

In the world of free will, some people choose to do wrong, and there are, unfortunately, victims of their choices. In other words, the responsibility for evil rests upon the person or persons who have decided to act in evil ways. Further, the Bible teaches that evil is personified in the form we call Satan, and he is the one, not God, who has come to kill, steal, and destroy.[3]

Isn't it interesting, however, that when victimization does happen to us, we are tempted to blame ourselves and God, instead of the perpetrator and Satan? That is backwards, a part of the lie that takes hold in victimization. In reality, God offers us his compassion and comfort when we have been victims of a spoiled world. He is the one who can empower us to recover and reach for better seasons in our lives.

CHAPTER 14

TREASURES
Revive Your Joy in Life

■

The season of recovery consists of a wide range of experiences and emotions. There will be peaks of faith and valleys of doubt. Just as a baby who is learning to walk takes two steps forward and then falls back a step, a recovering victim has moments when the intense feelings of anger, guilt, and doubt return.

A friend of mine who is a psychologist told me of a woman patient whose mother had refused to recognize her husband's physical and emotional abuse of her daughter. The daughter had been in successful therapy for a year when her mother refused to spend Mother's Day with her and her family. This rejection so vividly revived all the feelings of anger from the daughter's childhood memories that she attempted suicide, a drastic step back, but not a sign that she was not recovering. Her doctor reminded her of all the progress she had made so that she did not despair over this temporary regression, which was keyed by her childhood emotions.

Deep inside, each of us lives in a childlike world, and our emotions, our identities, and our pain are felt and experi-

enced at a childlike level. That world is not only one of difficulty and pain but also one of delight and pleasure. A
recovering person needs to revive the joy in life, which is
often associated with what the person treasures.

Each of us has a childlike definition of what we truly treasure in life and, like our identities in other respects, that
definition of treasure was formed during the earliest and
most critical stages of our development. Some of us still have
a childlike love of trains, planes, or boats, or the desire to be
a firefighter or a doctor. Others have the secret treasure of
wanting to be like Dad or Mom or a favorite uncle, or to
pursue a particular career goal, or to develop some personal
skill that has been inspired by important people in their
lives. Most of us have a childlike hunger for God and a desire
to be treasured by him and to please him.

A treasure is something that gives us enormous, childlike
delight, and which by itself can seem to make life worth-
while or which, by its absence, can make life seem empty. A
life lived to its fullest is a life that includes what is truly
treasured, no matter how simple that treasure may be.

For the victim, the subject of treasures is a troublesome
one. Because of feelings of ineligibility, the victim feels cut
off from whatever he truly treasures. The victim will sometimes fantasize about his treasures or see other people enjoying what he treasures, but he does so with a sadness that the
treasure is not for him. He may even take steps occasionally
in the direction of a treasure, but he will often be overcome
with feelings of unworthiness or the fear that if he embraces
what he treasures, he will have to pay for it by losing what he
wants in some other area of life. The result is one of either
living with no treasures at all or even adopting substitute
treasures. For a hurting person whose life doesn't seem to

make sense and who feels cut off from fulfillment in other ways, a hamburger can make the day! Many victims have come to the shocking realization that their isolation from the real world of pleasure and fulfillment has made compulsive behavior a treasure to them.

One of the goals of a season of recovery is to rediscover the delightful treasures of the child within. For some of us, this may be just as complex as getting in touch with the root of our pain, since many victims have repressed the reality of their treasures, just as they have repressed or forgotten their pain.

Nathan is a good example of what I'm describing. When I first met him, he was forty-two years old, married, and had three children. From all appearances, he was a successful and happy person. He was a pilot for a major airline, a cheerful and outgoing person; he seemed to have enough money to live comfortably and was deeply committed to God. Privately, however, he was a tormented person who was haunted by sexual compulsions and depression. My meeting with him and subsequent sessions with a professional counselor revealed that Nathan was a victim of childhood incest. Through counseling he began to understand the subject of treasures and their importance for his life.

"I have always enjoyed flying," he told me. "I've never been sorry I became an airline pilot, but in another sense I can't say I have enjoyed it like some of the other guys. In other words, I like it, but I could live without it, and I have seriously considered leaving the airlines and doing something else. The problem is, I can't decide what the something else should be."

"It sounds as if you are still trying to figure out what to be when you grow up," I said.

"Exactly," he agreed. "You wouldn't believe all the occupations I have tried. In my mind, I change my career almost every year."

As Nathan detailed some of the different jobs he'd had, I thought to myself, *He's a unique dropout. He either succeeds and then drops out or he pursues a degree and quits right after he's achieved it. What a guy!*

"Over a period of twenty years, I probably fooled around with at least twenty different hobbies," he continued. "One year I would be into golf, then the next year photography, and so on, but I never stuck with any of them. I would look at people who kept the same hobby for years, and I couldn't relate to them. Sometimes I would even feel guilty about it."

A crucial incident in Nathan's season of recovery stirred up the subject of treasures. "A friend of mine invited me to his mountain cabin for a weekend of fishing," Nathan said. "His cabin was about a three-hour drive from my house, and the road went through some beautiful rural country. The weather was spectacular. I was driving along, enjoying the whole scene and the freshness of what I had been discovering about my life when I saw a beautiful horse standing on an elevated portion of pasture. The palomino stood alone, silhouetted against the sky. I stopped, and while sitting in my car in the middle of the roadway, I burst into tears. Suddenly I felt as if I were five years old. I could hardly control the eruption of emotion and finally had to pull my car over to the side of the road.

"During that entire weekend, all I could think about was that horse, and whenever I did, I felt like crying."

"Were horses important to you when you were a child?" I asked.

"Yes," Nathan relied. "I loved them. I dreamed about

owning a horse or living on a ranch. I had visions of fishing trips on horseback and living my life as an old-fashioned cowboy."

"Did you ever ride horses when you were young?"

"I remember several occasions when I rode horses owned by friends or when I rented a horse to ride from time to time. But, Rich, it's really sad now that I reflect on the whole subject. There were times when I couldn't think of anything else but horses, but I also kept my distance from them. I remember seeing other kids who either owned horses or who were members of riding clubs and feeling jealous of them and sad that I would never be like them."

"Who told you they were different from you?" I asked.

"That's the tragedy. I don't remember anyone telling me that. My parents weren't opposed to my interest in horses. Nobody close to me was opposed to it. It was an assumption that was as real to me as blindness is to a person with no eyes.

"I remember when I was in college in a school that had a reputation for formal training in farming and ranching. I would look longingly at the students who were going to make a career out of working with horses. I couldn't imagine the joy of taking college courses with such a wonderful goal in mind."

"Didn't you ever consider that career for yourself?"

"That's what's crazy about this," Nathan replied. "I don't remember making any decision. I just acted as though the world of horses was one where I didn't belong, and I never seriously thought about investigating it. I lived as though somebody, somewhere, had already made that decision for me."

"What has changed in your life since this discovery?"

"A lot," Nathan said. "For one thing, I have realized how out of touch I've been with my true desires. I have looked back on my life and seen why it was sometimes so difficult to make decisions—seldom was one of my options anything I truly cared about.

"I have also allowed myself to embrace my love for horses. I took a riding class and loved every minute of it, and I'm making friends with people who love horses. I don't know where it is going to lead, but I can't put into words how much it has meant to me to admit to myself and others how much I like horses and how much I look forward to owning a horse. Who knows, maybe I'll invest in a horse ranch! I have even allowed myself to hang a beautiful painting of a palomino in my office at home, something I never would let myself do."

Nathan's story is one I have heard often from victims who are recovering and are allowing themselves to recapture treasures from which they previously felt disqualified.

NURTURING YOUR TREASURES

You might ask, "What should I do when I identify and embrace my treasures? Should I quit my job? Should I go back to school and pursue whatever it was that I loved? Should I get rid of the things in my life that are incompatible with my treasures?"

Some people will find themselves making radical changes when they embrace their treasures. I have known many who have changed careers as a result. It is not always practical or necessary to do that, however. Remember that one of the goals of the season of recovery is to live in the real world. That involves not only discovering whatever treasures exist in your real world but also wisely and practically pursuing them or realistically understanding why you may not do so.

If your dream was to be a doctor, for example, and you are already at a stage in life where it would not be practical to pursue that goal, you will have to be honest with yourself. Even when your heart says "yes" to a treasure, there may be practical reasons for not pursuing it. For most people, however, the reason they have not embraced their treasures is because they felt ineligible to experience the joy of having them. In this season of your life, you want to eliminate any of the emotional obstacles that stand between you and your treasure; you want to be able to wholeheartedly say yes regardless of the practical limitations.

Giving yourself permission to delight in your treasures and taking whatever modest steps you can toward nurturing that part of your life can lead toward significant healing.

TREASURES IN HEAVEN

A devout Christian might ask, "But aren't my treasures supposed to be heavenly? Shouldn't what I love have to do with my commitment to Christ?" I would say two important things in response to that. First, once we finally recognize God's love for us and are motivated by what Christ has done for us, there is no greater priority than knowing and serving him. If, as a Christian, you admit that anything or anybody in your life is more important to you than Christ, you need to reconsider your priorities. Following Christ is much like getting married. Before marriage, a career, hobbies, or other friends may delight your heart. After you fall in love and get married, you don't lose your interest in career, hobbies, or friends, but none of them should be more important to you

than the person you married. It is the same with our commitment to Christ. Nothing should delight me more than he
does, and nothing should be of greater importance than
he is.

It is interesting, however, that when we submit all our desires to God, he pays attention to those desires when he is
making assignments to us. In fact, we read in the Bible,
"Delight yourself . . . in the Lord, / And He shall give you
the desires of your heart."[1] So, even within the context of our
commitment to Christ and our desire to make him first in
our lives, a whole range of things delight us, some of which
God will provide himself. We need to make sure we are not
needlessly cutting ourselves off from our desires just because of the residue of victimization.

Secondly, the treasure for many committed Christians is
to know the Lord and to be in some particular position of
service and ministry. Instead, they deny this treasure in their
struggle for eligibility. As a minister, I have seen this on
numerous occasions. One man, in particular, stands out in
my memory. He had all the qualifications for church leadership and even the call of God to function in the pastoral role.
I gave him every opportunity to grow in those areas, and at
first, he eagerly accepted the opportunities. Inevitably he
would come to me and give a long, emotional explanation of
why he could not continue. Through talking with him, I discovered he was a victim. On the one hand, he felt the call of
God to ministry; on the other, he couldn't actually handle
being in a position of leadership or ministry because doing
so exceeded his sense of eligibility.

As you try to identify and embrace your treasures, remember you may have to do battle with guilt and fear. It is
almost as though the victim part of you erects the guilt and

fear to stand guard and prevent you from ever entering into the delight of your treasures. One woman I dealt with, who had a gruesome fear of flying on airlines, also had a treasure of wanting to travel and be an international missionary. Another person I counseled with, a young single woman, wanted to marry but was reluctant to enter into any potentially serious relationships and usually sabotaged them at some point because of feelings of ineligibility.

Identify your treasures! Embrace your treasures! Doing so is an important part of your season of recovery.

CHAPTER 15

FORGIVENESS
Choose Forgiveness Rather Than Revenge

■

I was driving on the freeways of Los Angeles one morning, searching the radio dial for something to occupy my driving time. I came across a popular talk show, and the subject was incest, so I tuned in. The guests were two women, both of whom had been victims of incest. One was a professional counselor and the head of an organization she had formed to provide support for incest victims. The other was a member of the organization and was there to share her personal story of incest. For about thirty minutes, the interview went well, and good information was shared. Then the host asked, "What should victims of incest do about their feelings toward the persons who did this to them?"

"We are increasingly encouraging victims to file lawsuits and take legal action against them," the counselor replied. "There needs to be some act of anger, some act of revenge that helps the victim regain control of life."

I was stunned. She went on to describe what amounted to personal campaigns of anger, which she felt victims should conduct against the people who perpetrated the victimization.

I couldn't disagree more.

For you, the victim, one important goal of a successful season of recovery is ultimately to adopt an attitude of forgiveness toward those who have been involved in causing your pain. Anything less than that will keep the pain alive and throbbing and will not accomplish anything productive for you or for the person who hurt you.

For many victims, the thought of forgiving those who caused their pain seems absurd and even impossible. Certainly forgiveness is contrary to the "get even" attitude of our society. It is an important step toward a more complete healing, however, which is one reason forgiveness was so paramount in the teachings of Jesus Christ.

Let me say a few things about forgiveness that I hope will be of help and encouragement to you.

FORGIVENESS DOESN'T HAVE TO BE THE FIRST THING YOU DO

Your season of recovery is a time to acknowledge what is true about you and about what you experienced. Part of that involves getting in touch with true feelings. Most of those feelings will not be good ones. But you cannot resolve those feelings without giving yourself permission to feel and acknowledge them, no matter how bad they seem to be. Some victims know that forgiveness needs to be their ultimate choice, and they feel guilty when they can't offer forgiveness from the beginning of their season of recovery. Their guilt, in my opinion, is unnecessary and unrealistic.

You don't have to forgive immediately. Recovery is a *sea-*

son and involves a lot of hard work. The goals of recovery are not achieved overnight. Some support groups or churches require victims to pray a prayer of forgiveness toward their victimizer the first time they acknowledge their pain. I think that is unwise. It isn't often that forgiveness is achieved in a short moment of wishing it to occur, and the victim almost always feels guilty when there are subsequent feelings of anger and hatred.

Forgiveness is a process. It takes time. And it is okay, even healthy, for victims first to acknowledge their feelings of *un*forgiveness.

WHY FORGIVE?

A point will come in your season of recovery when you have acknowledged your feelings and as much of the truth about what happened to you as possible. Then, to continue your healing, you will have to struggle with the issue of forgiveness.

"Why?" you may ask. "Why is it important for me to forgive? Why can't I just enjoy the hatred, the anger, and the feelings of wanting to take revenge?"

The following are several good reasons.

1. JESUS TELLS US TO FORGIVE

Jesus said that unless we are willing to forgive others, we will not be forgiven.[1] We are usually eager for God to forgive us, but we are often unwilling to forgive anyone who has wronged us. Even though you may be a victim, there are still issues and events in your life for which you need God's forgiveness, and you know it and feel guilty about it. God offers his forgiveness but warns that you will not experience the full benefit of being forgiven unless you are also willing to forgive others. You can't have it both ways.

2. FORGIVENESS AIDS YOUR RECOVERY

The chief reason for cultivating an attitude of forgiveness is that it will benefit you, not just the person you need to forgive. Revenge, anger, and hatred take their toll on the person feeling them. For you to live a life of unforgiveness is to choose to live in continued pain. You may say, "That person doesn't deserve to be forgiven, and I'm never going to do it." You are right. That person doesn't deserve forgiveness, but you deserve to experience the fruits of forgiveness. Let's face it. Why should you spend your life feeling guilt, anger, and bitterness and experiencing pain, disease, or even early death just because of the person who victimized you? Is that person worth it? Quite often, you are the only one carrying the pain, and your bitterness has no effect on the person who hurt you. If you can forgive, you will be released from unhealthy attitudes and feelings and will live a better life for it. *You deserve it!*

3. FORGIVENESS RELEASES THAT PERSON'S POWER OVER YOU

One goal of the incest victim I heard on the radio talk show was to overpower the person who hurt her so she would no longer be under his spell. I believe if you live a life of revenge and bitterness, you are continuing to be overpowered by the victimizer and by what happened to you. Your will to take revenge binds you like glue to the person who hurt you, even if that person is no longer part of your life.

Jesus once taught something that, at first, sounds confusing, but it illustrates what he was trying to accomplish in our lives. He told his followers, "Whoever compels you to go one mile, go with him two."[2]

At first reading, that sounds as if you are to submit willingly as a victim. The historical context may be helpful. In the days of Christ, Palestine was occupied by the Roman army. One law of the land was that if a Roman soldier requested a Jew to carry his pack, he was obligated to do so for one mile. No doubt, people resented the law and felt victimized by it. Then Jesus came along and said "Don't just go the required one mile, go two miles."

Why would he issue such an instruction? Wouldn't that tend to make his followers even more subject to bitterness? The answer is, no. What Jesus was essentially saying was, "For the first mile, the soldier has you under his control; you are trapped. For the second mile, you are under your own control and are walking in complete freedom from the law. In other words, for the first mile he has you. But for the second mile, you have him. It is an act of power, responsibility, and choice, and the result is freedom."

Do you see that if you elect to live your life confined and imprisoned by what has happened to you, you are trapped? For you to do the unexpected—to forgive your abuser—is to be free of him and what he has done to you.

FORGIVENESS DOESN'T MEAN
THE ABUSER WAS RIGHT

Many people think that to forgive someone means to pretend as though nothing bad happened and that nothing needs to be done about it.

I received a call on the radio one day from a woman I will

call Georgette. "I have been going through counseling to deal with the effects of molestation by my grandfather," she began. "I have come a long way, but one of the things that is making it harder for me is that I know he is also molesting one of my nieces right now, and I don't know how to handle that."

"Have you told your counselor about your niece?" I asked.

"No, because if I do, I know the counselor will report him and he will be arrested."

"That's precisely what needs to happen," I responded.

"But I have been wrestling with my feelings for him for a long time, and I have come to realize that he was a victim too. I think I am ready to forgive him for what happened to me. How could I forgive him and at the same time turn him in to the authorities?"

"I think you are misunderstanding forgiveness," I answered. "If you offer him your forgiveness, it means that you are offering him your understanding and that you are not going to put yourself in the place of God and try to personally punish him for what he did. In the same way that God has forgiven you, you are going to forgive him. That does not mean, however, that you are going to allow another person to get hurt or that you are going to prevent your grandfather from being held accountable for what he is doing."

"I can forgive him and yet turn him in?" she asked.

"Absolutely. You can come to a point of personal forgiveness and at the same time understand that it is right for him to be arrested and for your niece to be rescued. Justice is not based on hatred or unforgiveness. We don't put people on trial because we hate them, but because it is the healthy thing to do when someone has done wrong or is of harm to someone else.

"A friend of mine owns a cabin in the mountains," I continued. "One summer evening when the cabin was unoccupied, a burglar broke in and started ransacking the place. A neighbor saw what was going on and called the police, and the burglar was caught. The culprit turned out to be a young man in his early twenties who was hooked on drugs and had broken into the cabin looking for something of value to sell so he could use the money for drugs.

"My friend felt compassion for the young man and arranged to visit him in jail and to offer his forgiveness. At the same time, however, my friend agreed to press charges against the man and to require him to go through whatever the law required. The burglar was tried, convicted, and sentenced, and my friend went through every step of the process with the young man, because of the compassion he had developed for him.

"Eventually, the burglar served his time, went through rehabilitation, had a powerful experience with God, and is now actually working for the man whose cabin he broke into. That story is a good example of how we can truly forgive someone and, at the same time, require that person to be held accountable to God and to civil authorities for what he has done. My friend's decision to press charges and to see this young man go through the legal system was not an act of revenge. It was a commitment to do what he felt was right."

Forgiveness means that I am going to overcome the hypocrisy of crying out to God and others for understanding and forgiveness for my faults while not being willing to offer forgiveness to others. Forgiveness means I am not going to play God and take revenge against my enemies. Forgiveness does *not* mean that courageous decisions will not be made about my abuser's relationship with me, with others, or even with the law. Those decisions will be made based, not on hatred, but on what is right, healthy, and just.

CHAPTER 16

VICTIMS OF VICTIMS
Family Members and Friends Need Help

■

If you've fallen in love with a victim or have any family members who are victims, life for you can be a real adventure (to put it mildly). I sometimes tell the story about the man who went to his doctor and was told, "You have only six months to live."

The man sat down stunned and asked the doctor, "What am I going to do?"

The doctor said, "Well, if I were you, I'd find a nice young girl who is a victim and marry her."

"Marry a victim?" the man asked astonished. "Why would I want to do that?"

"It'll be the longest six months you've ever lived!" the doctor replied.

Many of you can say "Amen" to that!

The friends and family of deeply hurting people often need as much help and encouragement as the victim does. I would like to offer some advice that may be beneficial. What I have to say is directed to spouses of victims, but much of it can be applied to other relationships as well. If you are a

203

victim, you may be tempted to skip this chapter. Before you flip the page, however, read a little further. You might just understand your husband or wife or friends a little better if you see your problems from their perspectives.

REMEMBER THAT YOU ARE DEALING WITH A HURTING PERSON

Sometimes when we finally understand why a person acts a certain way, we are inclined to accept that person more easily. If someone close to you experienced a high fever, became delirious, and said things that sounded bizarre or even hurtful, you would probably dismiss what was said because of the fever. That doesn't mean you liked what the person said, and it doesn't mean you would allow that person, while sick, to do anything he or she feels like doing. But you would understand better what was going on.

To some extent, the situation is the same with a hurting person. You may not like that person's words and conduct at times, and you don't necessarily have to withhold your disapproval, but when you understand what contributes to such behavior and the extent of healing that needs to be experienced by the victim, you will have a different attitude toward the victim's actions. Once, after a seminar I conducted on victimization, a man I will call Hank came to me afterwards with tears in his eyes. He told me he never would view his wife exactly the same again.

"I have hated Carolyn for the way she has treated me," he confessed. "She is a wonderful woman in many respects, and I have loved her, but some of her behavior toward me and our children has been wrong."

"Like what?" I asked.

"For one thing," Hank said, "we have never had much of a sex life. At the least, she has never been very interested, and at the most, she has resented the fact that sex even exists. I have always interpreted her attitude as selfishness and rebelliousness on her part and have treated her pretty rotten as a result."

"How has your feeling changed?"

"Well, I still don't want to continue to live as we have been," Hank continued, "and I hope our sex life changes, but at least now I know why sex has been such torture for Carolyn. It is a direct result of her being repeatedly sexually abused by her grandfather when she was growing up."

"When did you find out about the abuse?" I asked.

"Not until recently. Carolyn had partially blocked it out of her mind, although she said she had flashbacks about it from time to time. I finally insisted that we seek counseling, and the counselor saw evidence that Carolyn was a victim and began working with her. Now that Carolyn has shared with me some of what happened between her and her grandfather and her feelings about it, I consider it a miracle that we have had any sexual relationship at all. As I said, I don't like the status quo, and I'm praying our life together will get better, but I can no longer hate Carolyn for our poor sex life."

THE MAGNETISM OF VICTIMS

One good reason for spouses and friends to offer understanding and compassion to the victim in your life is that many of you are victims yourselves!

That's right. Victims attract victims.

Often both partners in a marriage are victims, and that

fact is part of the dynamic that brought them together. So before you spend much time resenting the hurting person in your life, you should put some honest thought into why, of all the people you had to choose from, *you chose* that person as friend or spouse.

A business acquaintance of mine named Jason asked if he and I could get together for breakfast. "My wife, Charlotte, is a victim," he told me at the restaurant where we had agreed to meet, "and we both attended your seminar about victimization two weeks ago. You mentioned something about victims being attracted to victims."

"That's right," I replied. "It happens a lot."

"I've never thought of myself as a victim," Jason said, "but I've been thinking about what you said, and a clear pattern in my life seems to emerge."

"What kind of pattern?"

"I didn't get married until my thirties," Jason continued. "But I did have three or four serious relationships before then, and I lived with one of my girlfriends for about four years. I never put it all together until after your seminar, but now that I think about it, every one of my girlfriends was a victim. The girl I lived with for such a long time was sexually abused by her father, which is the same thing that happened to my wife, Charlotte. The interesting part, Rich, is that neither Charlotte nor I knew that when we married. She knew some awkward things had happened between her and her father, but she never thought of them as molestation and never told me anything about it."

"What do you think that means about you?" I asked.

"I don't know. That's what I wanted to ask you," he replied. "I know my father was an alcoholic, and we had some hard times when I was growing up as a child, but does that make me a victim too?"

"Jason," I said, "I'm not saying every person is a victim, but it is clear that you are attracted to women who are victims. Exactly what has contributed to that attraction, I don't know, but I have not met the child of an alcoholic yet who does not have some residue in his or her life that needs disposing of."

Typically, Jason tried to reject the implication of my statement. "Let's go back to Charlotte," Jason said. "She's got a lot of problems. I can see that now. But why did I choose her?"

"You will be the best one to answer that after you've thought about it for a while," I replied. "But there could be many reasons. One is eligibility. You remember at the seminar we talked about the five stages of a season of destruction, one of which was eligibility. We tend to look at all the people in our world and take the ones for whom we feel a comfortable eligibility. You saw from the beginning that Charlotte had some problems, but you also loved the good things about her. When all was said and done, you felt you were eligible for her and she for you.

"I also think there is the tendency for one hurting person to have special compassion for another hurting person. We often become 'rescuers' who discover value in trying to improve another person's life by marrying or befriending that person. This sounds loving and sacrificial, but the relationship is more that of nurse to patient than a commitment of friendship between two lovers.

"Many victims are also quiet and nondemanding on the outside, and sometimes their spouses have been attracted to them because they interpret that disposition as a sign of strength and stability. In fact, many times victims are attracted to that nonconfrontive personality because they want relationships with people who will not hold them accountable for their own problems.

"There are a lot of factors," I concluded, "and not all of them are simple to summarize, but it is often true that victims are attracted to victims."

"So what should I do now?" Jason asked.

"First, if there is resentment in your marriage, don't focus the blame on your wife. You must carry part of the responsibility for the fact that you are together and realize that, if you were not, you would probably be in relationship with somebody much like her. Work with her and encourage her to work with you to identify and overcome the problems in your lives. Make a commitment to do it together.

"You and Charlotte are both refugees from pain who have found yourselves in one another's arms, alternating between being attracted to one another and pushing one another away. If each of you can admit that the problems in your marriage are not simply the fault of just one person, if you can work together in your seasons of recovery, you'll come out of it with a bond to one another that can be very special."

EXPECT CHANGE

If you are married to a victim who is recovering, your relationship with that person will change. You might say to yourself, *Good, that's what I wanted—change!* But your spouse's getting well will have a significant effect on you, especially if you are a victim too.

To illustrate this, let me refer once again to the couple we just met, Jason and Charlotte. For most of their marriage, the focus of concern was on Charlotte because she seemed to have the most problems. Even though Jason didn't like living with Charlotte's problems, there was a payoff for him because he could live and act as though everything wrong in their home was her fault. As she recovered, however, their relationship began to change.

"I'll never forget the day," Charlotte said, "when I realized we were now having to work on Jason's problems, not just mine." They were like two wounded soldiers in a foxhole. The one most seriously hurt gets the most attention. Once that soldier is helped, however, the focus changes to the one still wounded.

Jason also admitted the change in their relationship. "I went through a time of feeling threatened by what was happening in Charlotte's life. Before she got help for her victimization, for example, she was not good at confrontation. As time went by, however, she was better able to express her concerns about me and about our home, and that was new for me. I wasn't sure I liked it!"

"Also, Charlotte had been overweight for as long as I had known her. One result of her recovery was her ability to control her eating. The more weight she lost, the more threatened I felt. I not only didn't feel eligible to be married to a sleek, good-looking lady but also feared losing her to someone else. In other words," Jason concluded, "Charlotte wasn't as safe to me anymore. She had learned to carry responsibility for herself and her feelings and to control her life. That was not the kind of woman I married."

If you are married to a person who is getting help, don't just bundle that person up and send him or her off to the counselor to "get fixed." The more successful that person's recovery, the more you will be required to be part of the process. Chances are, you will have to enter your own season of recovery as well.

YOU NEED SOMEBODY YOU CAN TALK WITH

Oftentimes the friends and family of victims need professional counseling just as much as victims, partly because they have been victimized by another person's victimization. Even if you don't see a professional counselor, you need somebody with whom you can honestly express your feelings. You are hurting too. You are angry too. You feel hopeless too. You need what some people call "a burden bearer."

When a victim is in the season of recovery, you need to be wise about the kind of relationship you have with that person. You may feel resentment, impatience, and occasional hopelessness, which should not be buried inside you but cannot be shared with the victim. Some people have formed burden-bearing groups that meet on a regular basis. A friend of mine, a physician, meets with a group of four good friends who eat breakfast together once a week. They have made a commitment to be honest with one another, and they have the freedom to say whatever they are feeling in that setting. My friend says the group helped change his life and his marriage.

REMEMBER THE WORD *SAFETY*

For most victims, all the skill, intelligence, talent, and knowledge they have is committed to one major project: avoiding threat and pain. The operative word in the life of the victim is *safety*. If you understand that and are sensitive to it, you may have a better chance of making successful decisions with that person. It sounds as if I am describing an incredibly fragile person—and I am!

The problem is, many victims don't seem as fragile as they are, and when those around them discover their fragility, they are always surprised. That is especially the case if the victim in your life has been an angry person, who has ruled your home and your relationship by that anger. Many victims have developed what appears from the outside to be confidence, control, maturity, and stability, and in some cases those qualities are truly present. However, the victim's childlike sense of fear needs to be understood. This was effectively expressed by two close friends of mine, Gene and Barbara, who were each seeking help for victimization.

"I could never figure Gene out," Barbara said. "He was a great guy in many respects, but we could never count on having a special weekend together or a night out for dinner or anything like that. I began to think of him as a very boring person."

"I really felt bad being such a spoilsport," Gene added, "but I never felt much like doing some of the things Barbara wanted to do. I would rather stay home."

"As Gene got in touch with some of what influenced his life," Barbara said, "it was clear that he had been emotionally beaten by his aunt, who helped rear him, and that anything other than being in the safety of his own home was a threat to him."

Gene added, "I never thought of it in those terms, but that was what was going on. I was making choices of safety. I didn't like anything that was being decided for me or required of me because it would make be suck in my breath in fear and think, *This feels out of control.*"

Slowly Barbara learned to adjust to Gene's response. "I

realized I shouldn't just 'make' the decisions about whether or not to go out to eat or to go on vacation, which was my habit, but go to Gene in undemanding ways and allow him to participate in the decision as much as possible. One year I suggested we fly to the east coast to see my parents, for example, and Gene nearly had an anxiety attack."

"That suggestion confronted many of my fears at once," Gene explained. "I was afraid of flying. I was afraid of being far from home. I don't like her parents, so I was afraid of being trapped for a couple of weeks in their home."

"How did you resolve that?" I asked.

"I decided not to put the pressure on," Barbara said. "I told Gene I would like to go, but that I would not force the issue. I encouraged him to think through the details of the trip and to choose whatever would be safe for him emotionally."

"After thinking about it," Gene said, "I wasn't so much afraid of being away from home as I was of flying, so I chose to go by train, which we both enjoyed. Also, I trimmed our stay at her parents' down to a week instead of two weeks, and I requested that we stay in a motel rather than in their home. That helped me feel I had a safe haven if I started feeling trapped."

"How did it go?"

"It wasn't perfect," Gene said, "but it was the most successful trip we have ever had."

I've heard similar comments from couples whose sexual relationship has been hindered because of one or the other's being a victim. One wife told me, "If my husband approaches me gently and holds me like a little child and comforts me and lets me know everything is okay, that releases me to respond to him sexually. If he doesn't do that, no matter how loving and sensuous he is, I start feeling that something out of my control is about to happen. I just close up inside!"

LEARN HOW A VICTIM CRIES "OUCH!"

Let's imagine you are working outside your home on a sunshiny day, perhaps raking leaves. Across the street you hear the sound of roller skates going up and down the sidewalk. Then there is an abrupt end to the sound, followed by a scream, and a sickening thud on the sidewalk. As you turn to look, you see a young girl lying on her back, sobbing as though not only her body hurts but her heart as well. What would be your first instinct?

I think most of us would want to do the same thing: run to the girl's side and investigate how badly she is injured, and then offer her some comforting arms in which to hurt and cry. Whenever we see somebody hurting, a normal response is to respond to and comfort that person.

Let me change the scenario a bit. Let's imagine again that you are outside on a sunshiny day, raking leaves, and the same little girl comes skating by, but she has a pea shooter and lands a lucky shot on your ear, which stings like fire. Then she comes skating by from the opposite direction and yells an obscenity at you. Finally, when she skates through your freshly raked pile of leaves and scatters them to the wind, you feel like wringing her neck and calling her a few names as well!

The significance of these stories is that, except for the girl's behavior and your reaction, everything else is the same. The setting is the same, the little girl is the same, you are the same, and *her hurting* is the same. In the first story, she cried in pain as a way of saying, "Ouch!" In the second story, she struck out in anger and hurtful behavior as a way of saying "Ouch!" In the second case, hers was an inner pain.

Many victims find themselves lashing out at those around them when they are feeling the worst about themselves. That is not justified behavior, and I am not suggesting it be considered acceptable. But if you are the unlucky person who is the target of such a display of emotion, it is valuable for you to think for a moment before you retaliate. Say to yourself, *This may be his way of saying, "Ouch!" He needs me to comfort and console him, not to get into an argument over the issue*. This response is difficult, but possible, as Ned, the husband of a victim, finally realized.

Ned and Jane had been married for more than twenty years before Jane dealt with the issues of victimization in her life. "We had lots of complex conflict in our marriage," Ned told me. "The issues we argued about were legitimate ones, but Jane's way of handling them was intense and out of control. We would end up arguing about her conduct more than the issues, and that frustrated her to tears."

Jane added, "I felt Ned wasn't taking me seriously. We had discipline problems with the kids, and I was constantly worried about the bills. Whenever I tried to express my frustration about those issues, however, we always ended up in conflict."

"One of the reasons," Ned said, "was that Jane was virtually incapable of communicating with me about her concerns. I don't remember a time when she said, 'I have something important we need to talk about.' Instead, she would give me the silent treatment for a few weeks, or

I would come home one night and find a raging, out of control woman on my hands. I resented that and, I guess, didn't try to hear what she was saying."

"And," Jane interjected, "I would become more frustrated as a result."

"The first improvement came when we started seeing our pastor for counseling, and he helped mediate some of our disputes," Ned continued. "He was the one who recommended we see a professional counselor, especially for Jane's victimization.

"One night I came home from work, and Jane was on a rampage. She had secluded herself in the bedroom, and when I walked in, she began raging about the finances. My first reaction was to be offended with the intensity and the manner of her reaction. I naturally wanted to defend myself from her accusations against me. I caught myself, however, and thought, *She's really hurting and is, in her own awkward way, crying out for comfort and encouragement. She doesn't need me to defend myself right now. She just needs me to listen.* I let her finish what she had to say, and then I walked over to her, took her in my arms, and said, 'I'm sorry it hurts so much.' She cried and cried and accepted my love and encouragement, and much to my surprise, we ended up making love. That wasn't even what I had in mind."

"Do you still react in some of the same ways?" I asked Jane.

"I'm working on it," she said, smiling. "I honestly didn't know how I was coming across to Ned and how counterproductive my reactions were. I felt so justified in how I was feeling that I didn't care much about anything else.

I've learned that Ned really isn't resistant to talking about problems as long as I don't begin the conversation with a nuclear explosion. We are learning how to communicate."

LEARN TO PERFORM TO A NEW AUDIENCE

Shakespeare said, "Life is a stage." In daily living, each of us is sometimes on a stage performing for those around us, and sometimes we are the audience for whom others perform. If you give someone a gift, you probably watch that person's reaction; you want to have the satisfaction of knowing the gift was appreciated. If that person "performs" to your expectation, you feel his gratitude. If not, the performance will be a disappointment to you.

In marriage, husbands and wives take turns performing in various ways for one another. Ordinarily, we can count on the person or persons for whom we are performing to be a good audience. Occasionally, however, especially in the families of victims, you find an unhealthy audience; you will find demands and expectations that are unreal and destructive. Then the person on stage needs to realize, "I can't afford to perform for this person anymore. I can no longer measure my performance by this person's reactions. No matter what I do, no matter how I perform, it isn't good enough."

Julie was a delicate-looking woman who did not look like the mother of six children. "I grew up in a violent home," she told me one day in my office. "My mother has always been an angry and difficult person, and I have hated that, but she still seems to have me under her spell. She calls me at least once a week and wants to talk for hours. Whenever I hear her voice, my stomach tightens, but I don't know what to do. She recently demanded that my husband and I allow her to take our four-year-old son on a three-week trip with her to another state. We don't want him to go, but when we tell her that, I'm sure she is going to call us names and threaten never to talk with us again."

"You've got to realize how destructive it is for you to measure yourself by her expectations," I told Julie. "Your mother has serious problems. She does not have a healthy relationship with you, and it is easy for you to react to her as a victim. She's not an audience you can perform for anymore."

"But I can't ignore her," Julie protested. "She is my mother, and things are not bad all the time."

"This is an important time of your life, Julie," I told her. "You are starting to make more decisions by yourself, without being influenced by your mother. That is good. What you are seeing is that you need to make those decisions on the basis of a different audience."

"What other audience do I have?" Julie asked.

"Most importantly, God," I replied. "Also, your own conscience. You need to decide what is the right thing to do about your mother, regardless of whether it fits her expectations. I suggest you sit down with a piece of paper and write what you think you need to do for your mother.

"For example, you might wish to send her a birthday card or a Christmas present each year, or you might realize you want to visit her once every three or four months or to call once a month. In other words, *you* select the ways you will express your love for your mother. Whether she is satisfied or not cannot be the measuring stick because she has already proven that her demands are unrealistic, and the prospects of pleasing her are bad."

There are no formulas, no simple rules, for helping those around us who are hurting from seasons of destruction, but having an understanding of the root of their pain and their behavior goes a long way toward knowing how to live with them.

CHAPTER 17

MARCHING TOWARD VICTORY!

■

Many victims have started triumphantly referring to themselves as "survivors," and I like that. Most victims I know have put more energy into everyday living than any nonvictim could ever comprehend. They have endured more pain and courageously conquered more obstacles than Olympic champions. The enormous skill that was developed for getting through ordinary hours and ordinary days would have earned them celebrity status if the world had been able to watch. Victims are truly survivors, with credentials that would rival those of any prisoner of war or marooned sailor.

As you make your way through your season of recovery, you can use those skills to pursue health and growth in your life instead of mere survival. You have the intelligence and the sheer willpower to have made it this far and under conditions that some people would have found unbearable. Now you can dedicate yourself to being set free.

Ask God for guidance and trust him for what you cannot do alone. Jesus promised that the Holy Spirit would lead us into "all truth," and that means *all* truth, the truth about ourselves and the truth about God.

Remember you are not aiming for perfection. The season of recovery is not another compulsive self-improvement project. Normal living includes times of pain and disappointment, loss and failure. When those times come, they do not mean you have failed to get well, but they may mean you are normal! I remember a remark made to me one day by a woman who had been a victim and who was now a new bride. She said, "I feel kind of depressed today because my husband and I are having financial problems." She said it as though she should not feel that way.

"Welcome to married life," I replied.

"Really?" she said, looking at me with surprise. "Is this the way I should feel?" She was so accustomed to being overwhelmed with the emotions of her victimization that she was thrilled to realize she might be experiencing what could be considered a routine bad day!

Get help. Don't remain alone and isolated in your pain. Victims tend to think, *I can handle this myself. It will be me and the Lord in my prayer closet, and we'll work it out.* The problem is, the only half of that partnership who is trustworthy is the Lord! Victims tend to be blind to what needs to be done to promote their healing and will defensively screen out even what the Lord is trying to say to them. The season of recovery is a process of learning the truth about you and the truth about God. Sometimes we need the skillful and wise counsel of another person to help us see the truth that we have previously not known or failed to see.

Let God redeem your pain! That's right, God can redeem and use anything that has happened in your life, no matter how bad. I don't know exactly how he does it, but I am enthusiastic about the fact that he does. The Bible reads, "And we know that all things work together for good to those who love God, to those who are the called according to his purpose."[1]

I recently talked with a woman named Pam about this during a weekend singles retreat. "My life seems like a waste," she told me. "I've lived in so much pain for so long that I feel robbed. Where has God been through all this?"

"I love a story from the Bible," I told her, "about when God's people demanded that he give them a king. God told them it was a bad idea, but they persisted, and he accommodated himself to their request. In other words, they rejected God's Plan A and chose their own Plan B.

"Later they realized what an astonishingly stupid thing they had done, and they were afraid God was going to strike them dead. Instead, God comforted them and told them not to be afraid. Because of their repentance, he was committed to them and wanted them now to promise to walk with him for the rest of their lives."

"How does that relate to me?" Pam asked.

"God not only forgave them and blessed them, but he somehow took the awful circumstances and made them part of his will. This kingdom, which was originated in sin and rebellion, became the same realm ruled over by King David and King Solomon, and if you follow the kingly line, it leads to Jesus Christ who is the King forever."

"You mean the kingdom we become part of when we accept Jesus is the same kingdom that began with that sin?" Pam asked.

"That's right," I answered. "Even though something

went terribly wrong, God made it wonderfully right, and he is able to do that with anything we are willing to entrust to him and ask him to redeem."

Pam started crying and said, "I am going to ask him to somehow do that with my life. I have always felt my life was such a mistake that God could never do anything with it."

"God never says, 'Oops,'" I told her. "Nothing is beyond his power, ability, and willingness to handle. He has turned Plan B into Plan A again for millions of people—and he can do it for you."

With God's strength you have survived. Now is the time to do more than survive. It's time to live!

N O T E S

CHAPTER 2

1. Grant L. Martin, *Counseling for Family Violence and Abuse* (Waco, TX: Word, 1987), 147.

2. Diana E. Russell, "The Incidence and Prevalence of Intrafamilial and Extrafamilial Abuse of Female Children," *Child Abuse and Neglect* 7:2 (1983), 133–46.

3. From an interview on "Talk from the Heart," March 1988.

4. David B. Peters, *A Betrayal of Innocence* (Waco, TX: Word, 1986), 20.

5. Martin, *Counseling,* 149.

CHAPTER 10

1. Matthew 18:3.

CHAPTER 11

1. Philippians 3:13–14.

2. Proverbs 28:13.

3. John 8:32.

CHAPTER 13

1. Romans 7–8.

2. Galatians 5:6–26.

3. Cf. John 10:10.

CHAPTER 14
1. Psalm 37:4.

CHAPTER 15
1. Matthew 6:14–15.
2. Matthew 5:41.

CHAPTER 17
1. Romans 8:28.